GANGS

OPPOSING VIEWPOINTS®

Other Books of Related Interest

Opposing Viewpoints Series

American Values
America's Children
America's Cities
America's Prisons
Chemical Dependency
Child Abuse
Civil Liberties
Crime and Criminals
Criminal Justice
Culture Wars
The Death Penalty
Drug Abuse
Economics in America
Education in America
The Family in America
Male/Female Roles
Mass Media
Poverty
Race Relations
Sexual Values
Social Justice
Teenage Sexuality
Violence
War on Drugs
Work

Current Controversies Series

Drug Trafficking
Gun Control
Hate Crimes
Police Brutality
Violence in the Media
Youth Violence

GANGS

OPPOSING VIEWPOINTS®

David Bender & Bruno Leone, *Series Editors*

Charles P. Cozic, *Book Editor*

OPPOSING
VIEWPOINTS®
SERIES

Greenhaven Press, Inc., San Diego, CA

Cover photo: Dave Allen

Greenhaven Press, Inc.
PO Box 289009
San Diego, CA 92198-9009

Library of Congress Cataloging-in-Publication Data

Gangs : opposing viewpoints / Charles P. Cozic, editor.
    p.   cm.
   Includes bibliographical references and index.
   ISBN 1-56510-363-7 (lib. ed. : alk. paper). —
ISBN 1-56510-362-9 (pbk. : alk. paper)
   1. Gangs. I. Cozic, Charles P., 1957– . II. Series: Opposing viewpoints series (Unnumbered)
HV6437.G36   1996
364.1'06'6—dc20   95-9015
                                              CIP

"Congress shall make no law . . .
abridging the freedom of speech,
or of the press."

First Amendment to the U.S. Constitution

The basic foundation of our democracy is the First Amendment
guarantee of freedom of expression. The Opposing Viewpoints
Series is dedicated to the concept of this basic freedom and the
idea that it is more important to practice it than to enshrine it.

Contents

Why Consider Opposing Viewpoints?

"The only way in which a human being can make some approach to knowing the whole of a subject is by hearing what can be said about it by persons of every variety of opinion and studying all modes in which it can be looked at by every character of mind. No wise man ever acquired his wisdom in any mode but this."

John Stuart Mill

In our media-intensive culture it is not difficult to find differing opinions. Thousands of newspapers and magazines and dozens of radio and television talk shows resound with differing points of view. The difficulty lies in deciding which opinion to agree with and which "experts" seem the most credible. The more inundated we become with differing opinions and claims, the more essential it is to hone critical reading and thinking skills to evaluate these ideas. Opposing Viewpoints books address this problem directly by presenting stimulating debates that can be used to enhance and teach these skills. The varied opinions contained in each book examine many different aspects of a single issue. While examining these conveniently edited opposing views, readers can develop critical thinking skills such as the ability to compare and contrast authors' credibility, facts, argumentation styles, use of persuasive techniques, and other stylistic tools. In short, the Opposing Viewpoints Series is an ideal way to attain the higher-level thinking and reading skills so essential in a culture of diverse and contradictory opinions.

In addition to providing a tool for critical thinking, Opposing Viewpoints books challenge readers to question their own strongly held opinions and assumptions. Most people form their opinions on the basis of upbringing, peer pressure, and personal, cultural, or professional bias. By reading carefully balanced opposing views, readers must directly confront new ideas as well as the opinions of those with whom they disagree. This is not to simplistically argue that everyone who reads opposing views will—or should—change his or her opinion. Instead, the series enhances readers' depth of understanding of their own views by encouraging confrontation with opposing ideas. Careful examination of others' views can lead to the readers' understanding of the logical inconsistencies in their own opinions, perspective on why they hold an opinion, and the consideration of the possibility that their opinion requires further evaluation.

Evaluating Other Opinions

To ensure that this type of examination occurs, Opposing Viewpoints books present all types of opinions. Prominent spokespeople on different sides of each issue as well as well-known professionals from many disciplines challenge the reader. An additional goal of the series is to provide a forum for other, less known, or even unpopular viewpoints. The opinion of an ordinary person who has had to make the decision to cut off life support from a terminally ill relative, for example, may be just as valuable and provide just as much insight as a medical ethicist's professional opinion. The editors have two additional purposes in including these less known views. One, the editors encourage readers to respect others' opinions—even when not enhanced by professional credibility. It is only by reading or listening to and objectively evaluating others' ideas that one can determine whether they are worthy of consideration. Two, the inclusion of such viewpoints encourages the important critical thinking skill of objectively evaluating an author's credentials and bias. This evaluation will illuminate an author's reasons for taking a particular stance on an issue and will aid in readers' evaluation of the author's ideas.

As series editors of the Opposing Viewpoints Series, it is our hope that these books will give readers a deeper understanding of the issues debated and an appreciation of the complexity of even seemingly simple issues when good and honest people disagree. This awareness is particularly important in a democratic society such as ours in which people enter into public debate to determine the common good. Those with whom one disagrees should not be regarded as enemies but rather as people whose views deserve careful examination and may shed light on one's own.

Thomas Jefferson once said that "difference of opinion leads to inquiry, and inquiry to truth." Jefferson, a broadly educated man, argued that "if a nation expects to be ignorant and free . . . it expects what never was and never will be." As individuals and as a nation, it is imperative that we consider the opinions of others and examine them with skill and discernment. The Opposing Viewpoints Series is intended to help readers achieve this goal.

David L. Bender & Bruno Leone,
Series Editors

Introduction

"Do young people make rational choices whether to join a gang or are they pushed to join by their social and economic circumstances?"

Ruth Horowitz, Gangs in America, 1990

In the 1920s, sociologist Frederick M. Thrasher conducted a landmark seven-year study of more than one thousand Chicago gangs. In his subsequent book, *The Gang*, Thrasher warned, "The boy with time on his hands, especially in a crowded or slum environment, is almost predestined to the life of the gang."

Thrasher discovered Chicago to be a virtual laboratory for his research. Gangs proliferated throughout "a broad twilight zone" of crowded inner-city slums, factories, and railroads, and among many ethnic groups—blacks, Hispanics, and whites, including European immigrants. The gangs' activities, whether committed out of economic need or for enjoyment, ranged from roughhousing and shooting dice to serious crimes such as drug dealing, hijacking, and murder.

Thrasher described an assortment of motivating factors leading largely disenfranchised and impoverished youths to become involved with gangs: broken or poor families, deteriorating neighborhoods, thrill-seeking, and admiration of older gang members.

Decades later, these same factors continue to attract children and adolescents throughout America to gangs. According to University of Southern California psychiatry professor Richard C. Cervantes, "These kids join gangs to fill certain needs like respect, loyalty, protection, economic opportunities, and emotional and social support." Such needs are especially great in inner cities, where poverty, violence, and marginalization afflict young people, Cervantes and others argue. Although youth gangs (definitions of which vary among jurisdictions) cross all class and race lines, most public concern focuses on violent minority males caught up in inner-city drug dealing and turf wars.

The reasons why youths join gangs can be divided into two categories, those involving free choice and those involving little or no choice. The first type applies to those who, of their own free will, join a gang to satisfy their ego or greed. What these young people seek, and often crave, includes material gain, prestige and respect among peers, and thrills.

"Figalo," a 31-year-old former Latin King gang member from Chicago, depicts the lure of wealth that entices many adolescents: "Stories of 15-year-olds driving BMWs, Cadillacs, and Mercedes Benzes with trunks full of weapons and pockets stuffed with thousands of dollars are as common as they are true." Such accounts have convinced many inner-city youths that drug-dealing and other gang activities are sure ways of gaining money and esteem.

Sociologist Martin Sanchez Jankowski, who over a ten-year period studied gangs in Boston, Los Angeles, and New York, agrees that the allure of money is a powerful incentive for gang membership. Jankowski argues that joining a gang is part of a rational decision-making process by which, after weighing alternatives, youths seek to reap the rewards and advantages gangs offer. He argues, "They could join other groups in the neighborhood, but they join gangs." Such individuals, Jankowski adds, can more readily satisfy their needs within a gang structure than on their own.

A related attraction is the thrill of, and power concomitant with, being a gang member. According to FBI agents Alan Brantley and Andrew DiRosa, "It appears that gangs fulfill a need essential to many youths—excitement. Interviews with gang members often reveal a fascination with firearms." For those youths who feel a sense of powerlessness, the agents argue, "guns are the quickest and surest route to empowerment."

Besides these free-choice reasons, experts identify a wholly separate category of factors—socioeconomic and environmental influences—attracting youths to gangs. According to Felix M. Padilla and James Diego Vigil, who studied gangs in Chicago and Los Angeles, respectively, joining a gang is more often a conditioned response to the experience of growing up in inner cities than a free choice. Joining a gang is a predictable consequence, the pair maintain, for youths surrounded by unemployment and poverty, an entrenched gang subculture (including friends or relatives who are current or former gang members), and dangerous levels of crime and violence.

According to Padilla and Vigil, among others, few inner-city youths grow up unaffected by these influences. For example, Vigil has studied succeeding generations of Chicano gang members in East Los Angeles and their effect on children. Vigil writes in *Barrio Gangs*, "Peer and veterano [veteran gang member] models were cited [as influences by interview subjects] on a regular basis, and always the young boy wanted to measure up to the 'war' stories."

Many such youths may view gang membership as an

inevitable phase or part of life or believe that there are no other options but to join a gang. As one 18-year-old member of Chicago's Black Disciple Nation told the *New York Times*:

> Around here, if you're not in a gang, [people] still think you're in a gang. You can't walk to school. You can't go where you want, when you want, so you might as well be in a gang. Then at least when trouble starts, you ain't by yourself. You got some aid and assistance. You got a chance to live. If I didn't have to, I wouldn't be in no gang.

Whatever their reasons for joining gangs, many gang members believe that eventually they will be either imprisoned, seriously injured, or killed. Indeed, a sense of doom is evident in some young people's clothing, inscribed with slogans such as "Shoot me, I'm already dead." What many communities fear is that these attitudes will spread to younger children who idolize or seek to emulate gang members.

Although the temptation may be great, gang involvement is not an inevitable outcome for inner-city youths. Regardless of whether a strong gang subculture exists in certain neighborhoods, many youths successfully avoid gangs. As Walter B. Miller writes in *Gangs in America*, "Pressures to leave or not to join gangs are in many cases supported by community antigang pressures" from parents and former gang members themselves.

The authors in *Gangs: Opposing Viewpoints* consider the influences drawing youths to gangs as they assess America's gang problem in these chapters: What Encourages Gang Behavior? How Serious a Problem Are Gangs? How Can Street Gangs Be Controlled? Personal Narratives: How Do Gang Members View Themselves? Whether Americans consider gang members as predatory criminals or disenfranchised youths, this anthology can provide them with a better understanding of the complex phenomenon of gangs.

What Encourages Gang Behavior?

Chapter Preface

Ever since Frederick M. Thrasher's landmark study of 1,313 gangs in Chicago during the 1920s, researchers have explored why gangs are formed, what motivates gang activity, and why so many youths are drawn to gangs.

Many gang members claim they are attracted to gangs out of a need for protection. Indeed, this need was cited as the impetus for the creation of the Crips gang in Los Angeles in 1971. According to Stanley Williams, a cofounder of the gang,

> There were so many gangs prevalent during that era, and in our neighborhoods, that we had to band together against them to protect each other and to protect our family members, our loved ones, and to create an atmosphere in our communities where it would be safe for all of us.

However, what began as violence-for-protection evolved into more random and rampant violence. "Slowly but surely . . . Crips violence had run amok," Williams recalls. "It was more about flexing your muscles. We were hurting our own kind."

Like Williams, many inner-city youths perceive joining a gang as more of a survival technique than a choice. But there are other forces at work attracting youths to gangs and driving gang crime and violence. The viewpoints in the following chapter examine these factors.

"[Gangsta Rap] coerces, influences, encourages and motivates our youth to commit violent behavior, use drugs and abuse women."

Gangsta Rap May Encourage Gang Behavior

C. DeLores Tucker

C. DeLores Tucker is the national chairwoman of the National Political Congress of Black Women, a lobbying group in Washington, D.C. In the following viewpoint, from her February 23, 1994, testimony at a U.S. Senate hearing on violence and popular music, Tucker argues that the lyrics and images in "gangsta rap"—rap music performed predominantly by young blacks emulating gang members—poisons the minds of inner-city youths and glamorizes and encourages crime, violence, vulgar language, and abuse of women. Tucker proposes, as a preventive measure, banning the sale of obscene gangsta rap music to minors.

As you read, consider the following questions:

1. What does Tucker blame for the proliferation of obscenity and violence in popular music?
2. At what point does popular music become destructive of community standards, according to Tucker?
3. What does the author propose that government do to build youths' skills?

From C. DeLores Tucker's statement to the U.S. Senate Judiciary Committee's Subcommittee on Juvenile Justice, February 23, 1994.

Npcbw [National Political Congress of Black Women] is not against rap or hip hop. To the contrary, we support and encourage the artistic creativity of our young people. We love our young people. However, we are against "Gangsta Rap" and misogynist lyrics. As African American women, we are especially aware of the social and economic conditions that have spawned some of this behavior. Those of us, which includes over sixty major national organizations, who have taken up the mantle of this crusade to save our children have been arduously working to eliminate the *root causes* of the social ills plaguing our communities. We see this battle against the negative effects of Gangsta Rap as an important element in our struggle to uplift the African American community and America as a nation.

If Dr. Martin Luther King, Jr., the moral leader and conscience of the nation during his time, were alive today, he would be leading a nationwide crusade against Gangsta Rap. Dr. King would be marching and demonstrating against the glamorization of violence and its corrupting influence, which have now become a part of our culture in the name of freedom. This freedom—freedom from responsibility and accountability—is not the kind of freedom that Dr. King risked his life for. Indeed, Dr. King would be deeply saddened by such a misuse of freedom of speech. As Coretta Scott King said in her 1994 State of the Dream address: "Young people often look to performing artists for moral guidance and inspiration as well as entertainment, but when these artists glorify guns and beatings, they are injecting poison into the veins of America's future."

Enough is enough! I am here today to put the nation on notice that the proliferation of violence and unacceptable sexual messages in our youth's music is due in large part to the avarice of the record industry. *The record industry is out of control!* Some $780 million worth of rap records were sold in 1993, with more than half of the purchasers being under the age of 17, and 50 percent of those minors were between the ages of 10 and 14 years old. Something must be done to stop the financing and promoting of this cultural plague that is infecting the minds of our most valuable asset—our children.

It is our moral responsibility to halt the sale of this pornographic rap. It teaches our children to rape, kill and do acts of violence against their people. This misogynist rap further dehumanizes and disrespects all African American women by calling us bitches and ho's.

The Impact of Gangsta Rap

First, I want to address the issue of the impact of the Gangsta Rap lyrics and images on the youth of America. The misogynist lyrics that glorify violence and denigrate women are nothing

18

more than pornographic smut! This pornographic smut being sold to our children coerces, influences, encourages and motivates our youth to commit violent behavior, use drugs and abuse women through demeaning sex acts.

Our youth's constant exposure to these menacing images lowers their sensibilities towards violent behavior—making killing and abuse commonplace and acceptable. The acceptance of violence among our youth is leading to a devaluing of human life.

Gangsta Rap's Messages

Perhaps the most important element in gangsta rap is its messages, which center largely around these ideas: that women are no more than "bitches and hos," disposable playthings who exist merely for men's abusive delight; that it's cool to use any means necessary to get the material things you want; and most importantly, it's admirable to be cold-blooded and hard. . . .

Apparently, many rappers believe their own hype, and some don't hesitate to act on what they sing about. Look at:

• Tupac Shakur, arrested in Atlanta for shooting two cops.

• Flavor Flav, shooting at a guy he suspected of having sex with his girlfriend.

• Snoop Doggy Dogg, charged in connection with a murder, who says he packed two guns as "a protection thang."

Other rappers have faced charges for rape, shootings and assorted other crimes. I can't condemn them for getting into trouble, because I've been there myself. But I keep worrying about those kids who can't tell the difference between music and reality, and how this may affect them.

Nathan McCall, *The Washington Post*, November 14, 1993.

As a result, the reality of the nineties is that the greatest fear in the African American community does not come from earthquakes, floods or fires, but from violence. The kind of violence that has already transformed our communities and schools into war zones, where children are dodging bullets instead of balls and planning their own funerals. In fact, 94 percent of the Black youth that are killed today are killed by other Black youth.

In addition to the proliferation of violent behavior, the music inculcates in our youth false and hateful concepts about women at a tender age when it makes a profound impact on their outlook on life. We must not forget that music is a powerful learning tool inasmuch as it incites emotionalism and fosters memorization. If music does not contribute to the learning process, why is the music education approach of the "Hooked on Phonics" company so profitable and successful? Thus, this Gangsta Rap music can be seen as inappropriately educating our children.

Dangerous Messages

It is an unavoidable conclusion that Gangsta Rap is negatively influencing our youth. This explains why so many of our children are out of control and why we have more Black males in jail than we have in college. As an illustration of this, let me share with you excerpts from a letter that I received from a prisoner in Lorton, Virginia:

> Rappers . . . made it sound so good and look so real (that) I would drink and smoke drugs just like on the video . . . thinking that was the only way I could be somebody. . . . My hood girls became ho's and bitches. What's so bad is that they accepted it. You know why? Because they put themselves in the video, too, and the guns, money, cars, drugs, and men became reality. Look where this kind of thinking has gotten me . . . facing 25 years to life in jail.

We have seen incidents which vividly demonstrate the cause and effect correlation between what young people hear in rap and how they act. In one case, a 16-year-old from New Mexico, along with two of his friends, stabbed to death the boy's 80-year-old grandparents in a dispute over beer. A lieutenant investigating the case said that the teenagers worked themselves up by listening to a tape of Snoop Doggy Dogg entitled "Serial Killa." A second incident occurred in February 1994, when an 11-year-old Dayton, Ohio, boy accidently killed his 3-year-old sister and injured another 5-year-old sister while brandishing a gun and imitating the actions of Snoop Doggy Dogg.

In addition to fueling these atrocities, Gangsta Rap has contributed to the lowering of the standards of social behavior among our youth. Because Gangsta Rap has glorified and made popular the use of vulgar language, our youth are routinely referring to each other in disparaging terms and infusing their everyday conversations with profanity. Because of their immaturity, they are not aware that this language is socially unacceptable in all other circles.

Parents and Officials Should Be Concerned

Even if a direct link cannot be made between today's violence and Gangsta Rap, parents and elected officials need to be seriously concerned about Gangsta Rap because it is obscene and sexist; it is driven by racism and greed; and it is ultimately destructive of community mores and values.

As I see it, the first three things to note about Gangsta Rap are

1. It is obscene! 2. It is obscene! 3. It is obscene!

Take a look at the lyrics. The vulgarity is overwhelming, even for many adults. Take a look at the graphic artwork that is sold with Snoop Doggy Dogg's album *Doggystyle* (which any child can purchase in a record store). If the filth that is depicted in those cartoons is not obscene, then I submit that nothing is.

Obscenity has long been an exception to free speech. As U.S. District Judge Jose Gonzalez explained in his June 1990 opinion on the 2 Live Crew case [declaring one of the rap group's albums obscene]:

> Obscenity is not a protected form of speech under the U.S. Constitution, with or without voluntary labeling. It is a crime. . . . Violation of the laws against obscenity is as much against the law as assault, rape, kidnapping, robbery or any other form of behavior which the legislature has declared criminal.

Racism and greed are the sustaining forces behind Gangsta Rap. It is no coincidence that the characters displaying the most indecent behavior for all the public to see are African Americans. Some argue that these artists are merely speaking frankly about *their reality* and the Black cultural experience. But, as Dr. Benjamin Hooks, former executive director of the NAACP [National Association for the Advancement of Colored People], noted, "Our cultural experience does not include debasing our women, the glorification of violence, the promotion of deviant sexual behavior." This type of music is widely aberrant from the great music and musicians born of our culture and which have graced America.

African Americans have historically been victims of the blatant lie that we, as a race, are dishonest, lazy, women-hating, violent, gun-toting people. Human decency does not and never has had the slightest thing to do with one's racial background or even one's physical environment.

Record Companies' Greed

An example of how racism is undergirding Gangsta Rap can be seen in the experiences of rapper Lichelle "Boss" Laws. As the *Wall Street Journal* article of February 3, 1994, reported, when her style of rap was considered soft, she was told that she would not be produced unless her rap became hardcore and she used profanity. This has been true for many African American artists seeking record contracts. Placing profit ahead of social obligation, record companies routinely market music which glorifies violence, demeans women, glamorizes the usage of illegal drugs and even crosses the line into being audio pornography. This points to the other vice prevalent in the Gangsta Rap industry, and that is greed. It is almost a billion-dollar facet of the recording industry, generating a wealth of products from CD's to fashion, from t-shirts to films, even fueling the success of other industries such as malt liquor and firearms. In light of this, the greed that fuels Gangsta Rap today makes the worst Black exploitation film of the seventies seem tame by comparison.

This greed is taking the artistic elements out of rap music. As written in *Billboard* magazine:

> Art is a personal expression of the honest reach toward one's ideals. It strives toward the deeper, dimensional truths no mirror can hope to convey. It is a creative exploration and reaffirmation. . . . If a given expression does not . . . embody these qualities, then it is not art; instead it may be . . . at worst, a device for manipulation in the service of material gain.

Lastly, another reason for elected officials to be concerned about the influence of Gangsta Rap is that it can have the long-term effect of undermining our social order. By promoting and constantly depicting the type of behavior synonymous with Gangsta Rap, society is validating antisocial behavior.

As printed in *Billboard*, this

> leads to the death of conscience, the corruption of the spirit, and ultimately the destruction of the individual and the community. Whenever a culture condones or accommodates such practices because of their lucrative aspects, or pretends they can be isolated or ignored, then the inherent falsehoods can flourish.

This can result in the downfall of the society.

> No one form of popular music is important enough to justify or excuse racism, sexual bigotry, and the endorsement of sociopathic violence.

Government Must Intervene

At what point does this art form become actively destructive of community standards? When the recording crosses the line into pornography. When violence and sexual acts or body parts are graphically spoken of or depicted in videos. At the point when these things occur, then the full authority of government should be used to restrict access of such music and videos to minors. In particularly egregious instances, Congress should put forth measures to remove the offending product from the marketplace. . . .

Short-term fixes [such as more law enforcement and prisons] will do nothing to improve the lives of children like the nineteen that were removed from a home in Chicago in February 1994 because of parental neglect and abuse. They are prime examples of the children that Gangsta Rap will influence. Because of the lack of positive influences, their minds will be fertile and receptive ground for internalizing the violence glorified in Gangsta Rap. Children such as these, our most neglected population, will become a social time bomb in our midsts. Being coaxed by

Gangsta Rap, they will trigger a crime wave of epidemic proportions. Regardless of the number of jails built, it will not be enough! Neither will there be enough police nor quick-fix government programs to contain the geometric explosion of crime. We as a nation must act now and we must act decisively.

The solutions that I am suggesting require that we think in terms of curtailing crime at its earliest stages by investing in our youth. As a weapon to combat today's violence, Congress needs to establish public/private partnerships which create live-in schools patterned after the Milton Hershey School in Hershey, Pennsylvania, the Stephen Girard College in Philadelphia and the Father Flanagan Boy's Town in the Midwest. These facilities provide a wholesome and educational home and school environment free of violence.

In addition, since the government is in the process of downsizing the military, Congress should now examine the idea of converting these military bases into training academies for first- and second-time youth offenders. These bases could be put to good use by giving youth the skills they need to be productive citizens, rather than jailing them and giving them no ability to discontinue a life of crime.

Banning the sale of Gangsta Rap to our children is one preventive action Congress can take to curb violence. But it is one that is imperative to begin the process of healing our nation. *No one* and *no industry* should be allowed to continue the social and psychological poisoning of the young minds of this nation that is occurring with Gangsta Rap!

"Drug-related homicides and the feuding between rival gangs for control of drug markets have become a notable feature of all our large metropolitan centers."

The Narcotics Trade Incites Gang Violence

James M. O'Kane

Many Asian, black, Hispanic, and other gangs are key traffickers in drugs such as cocaine, heroin, and marijuana. In the following viewpoint, James M. O'Kane argues that in cities throughout America, ruthless ethnic gangs regularly use violence to intimidate rivals and protect their drug domains. O'Kane contends that the public's high demand for drugs promises to sustain vicious ethnic gang violence. O'Kane, a sociology professor at Drew University in Madison, New Jersey, was raised amidst crime and gangs in Brooklyn, New York, in the 1940s and 1950s and has had a lifelong interest in studying ethnic gangs.

As you read, consider the following questions:

1. According to O'Kane, what pattern does intraethnic gang violence take?
2. How does O'Kane describe the transition among the new ethnics from common street crime to organized crime?
3. In the author's opinion, how are some black gangs modeling themselves after underworld predecessors?

Today's mafia is no longer the threat it once was. The ever-growing Italian-American middle class no longer admires nor nurtures the mafiosi who are often old, infirm, and unable to replenish their ranks. Today's Italian middle class sees its children and grandchildren emulating doctors and lawyers rather than the gangsters that some Italian Americans had earlier taken as models. These once formidable "dons" and "capos" now spend their days either in federal prisons or in court contesting federal prosecutors. Their vaunted hegemony over poor neighborhoods has passed to other groups who now control the supply of the forbidden narcotic fruits—Jamaican marijuana posses, Colombian cocaine hidalgos, Chinese heroin triads, Dominican crack crews. Mafia mobs are no match for these new, vicious ethnic upstarts. . . .

Drugs and narcotics are to the 1990s what liquor was to the 1920s—tabooed substances, highly desired by many Americans. They offer their users euphoric highs, release from tensions and stress, and the chance to engage in something exciting, rebellious, and criminal. Their very illegality guarantees an extremely lucrative situation for organized crime, offering a market likely to continue and expand, for there is no realistic political movement to legitimate their manufacture, sale, and use as had been so with alcohol in the Prohibition era. Politicians also may find drugs potentially attractive: their sale and protection provide a possible source of campaign funds; they provide a method of making the underclass less of a problem since drug income fuels the underground economy of virtually all our impoverished inner-city neighborhoods even as it robs them.

Prohibition lasted but thirteen years until the Twenty-First Amendment rescinded it in 1933. Widespread drug use has been apparent for the past thirty years and its end is nowhere in sight. On the contrary, the use of certain drugs, such as marijuana, cocaine, crack, and speed by segments of the middle class implies that new potential markets are available and the new ethnic criminals are more than eager to exploit these opportunities risking everything, including their lives, to get a chance to "make it big" in America.

Drugs and Bloodshed

The results of this transition from Italian mobs to black, Hispanic, and Asian mobs are apparent everywhere. No one ethnic group is in charge. We witness the never-ending nightmare of carnage in the cities. In the poorest areas, the once stabilizing forces of family, church, school, community, and even neighborhood gang have disintegrated. The alienated youths in these areas join with similarly disaffected peers—often mere acquaintances—as they roam in wolf packs in "wilding" sprees seeking their prey. Bereft of stable criminal role models, they do the despicable deeds we see on the nightly news. Beholden only to themselves rather than to an organization, they lust for power and status, viewing competitors as deadly rivals.

Warlords appear, gain local notoriety, and are quickly gunned down; new leaders appear and a new cycle of internecine violence begins with drug dealers competing for prominence in a criminal realm without any clear codes of behavior. Today's drug pushers and steerers are tomorrow's drug czars. An Al Capone or a Lucky Luciano [infamous Prohibition-era mob bosses] has not yet emerged to impose a peace. Instead each ethnic minority battles within itself for a share of the spoils. Black drug dealers kill other black dealers; so also do Puerto Rican, Colombian, Chinese, Mexican, Jamaican dealers turn against their ethnic peers. . . .

A Harsh and Dangerous Trade

Like nations that stock an oversupply of nuclear weapons in the interests of deterrence, gang members need to present an impenetrable exterior to those seen as threatening their status, honor, or economic advantages, especially when they are marketing drugs.

The drug trade is harsh and dangerous, and others in the trade are more threatening than the police, who arrest but do not usually kill or maim. Nor does the drug trade routinely bestow the easy money so often portrayed by the media. Lower-rung dealers do not drive BMWs, wear gold jewelry, and get rich quick. They work round the clock, six or seven days a week, for low wages, often enforced by threat of violence.

Jerome H. Skolnick, *The American Prospect*, Winter 1992.

City after city reported increases in drug-related homicides in the late 1980s. Miami, for example, reported that 24 percent of its murders were related to narcotics and that 72 percent of these murder victims did *not* have drugs in their bodies at the time of their murder, implying that these deaths were "business-related" crimes. In 1986, 50 percent of all those murdered in Manhattan died in drug-related situations. Drug-related homicides and the feuding between rival gangs for control of drug markets have become a notable feature of all our large metropolitan centers. . . .

Upward Mobility

[A] few new ethnics have "made it" beyond the world of common street crime, graduating from burglary, mugging, thievery, assault, rape, murder, and so on, entering the more rational world of organized gang activity. Their tactics and felonious deeds may be the same as before, but the gang channels them toward its established ends that invariably further the power, prestige, and income of the gang and its members. Thus murders are committed in order to realize the gang's goals of increasing profits, controlling renegade members, protecting existing territories and markets, and terrorizing competitors. The crimes of ethnic newcomers become organized crimes governed by rational patterns and motives.

Having moved beyond common nonorganized street crime, these gangsters enter the realm of intraethnic gang rivalry where they contend, often violently, with similar newcomers from their own ethnic group for the spoils of narcotics trafficking. Their primary aim rests in consolidating their own power and the power of their gang. This entails the elimination and neutralization of fellow ethnic competitors. A casual reading of newspaper accounts of drug-related homicides reveals this daily intraethnic conflict where the violence often appears incomprehensible to both police and public alike. Competitors are executed in bizarre ways and oftentimes family members and innocent bystanders are similarly murdered. Yet this viciousness is a planned terror calculated to intimidate ethnic rivals into submission. It serves notice to the local community and competing criminals within the neighborhood that no opposition will be accepted.

Brutality Equals Success

The more cunning and brutal the gang, the better its chances of success, for no quarter is rendered in these local massacres. Their leaders gain prominence and status and are feared by both criminals and the public. . . . In their pursuit of power, current ethnic gangsters clearly match the vicious violence of their predecessors of past eras. Howard Blum reported [in the *New York Times* in 1978] on a South Bronx drug war between three Puerto Rican gangs that resulted in twenty-seven murders over a two-year period. . . .

The solutions of all twenty-seven homicides and the convictions of the killers scarcely dented the drug traffic, for new ambitious Hispanics quickly moved in and took over the territory. The only thing that continued to change were the names of the victims.

Black inner-city neighborhoods witness similar drug-related violence, frequently involving control of the ever-expanding crack market. A derivative of cocaine, crack presents newcomer criminals—particularly African Americans—with a golden opportunity for advancement in the underworld and the stampede of black gangsters seeking such stature has resulted in hundreds of killings. In New York City the degree of violence reaches bizarre proportions. In 1989 a twelve-year-old boy was kidnapped on his way to school and held for ransom by abductors seeking $500,000 from the boy's brother—a reputed middle-level crack dealer. A day later, the kidnappers cut off the boy's right index finger and mailed it with an audio tape that recorded the victim's frantic pleas to his mother. The ransom of $350,000 offered by the family was never accepted. A month later the boy's brother was murdered execution-style; a few weeks later the twelve-year-old's body was discovered by police who theorized that the entire incident was related to the crack trade.

Chicago provides further illustrations of drug-related violence. The Blackstone Rangers, an adolescent street gang in the 1960s and 1970s, has evolved into an adult gang, El Rukns, with loose ties to Black Muslims and which is, according to the F.B.I., "a violent criminal organization involved in narcotics trafficking and other illegal enterprises." In 1987, most of its leadership, including its founder, Jeff Fort, were convicted in federal court of conspiring to commit terrorist acts on behalf of the Libyan government, and in 1991 its remaining leadership faced narcotics, racketeering, and murder charges.

Jamaican criminals have organized narcotic networks in at least fifteen major American cities. The resultant internecine warfare among Jamaicans, and between them and American-born blacks, was responsible for 300 to 400 murders in the late 1980s. In 1987 in the *New York Times*, George Volsky cited James Brown, special agent of the Miami district of the Federal Bureau of Alcohol, Tobacco, and Firearms, who stated that Jamaican mobs— "posses"—have been identified in New York, Philadelphia, Hartford, Boston, Toronto, Washington, Miami, Fort Lauderdale, Cleveland, Chicago, Kansas City, Dallas, Houston, Denver, and Los Angeles. In December 1987, a shootout at a Brooklyn social club between rival Jamaican posses left two dead and more than a dozen injured. The best organized and most prominent of these posses is the Shower Posse based primarily in New York and Miami; other posses include the Dog Posse, the Tel Aviv Posse, the Spangler Posse, the Dunkirk Posse, the Water House Posse, and the Banton Posse. The main business of these posses is narcotics trafficking, particularly crack trafficking.

Many of these Jamaican gangsters are associated with the Rastafarian religious cult and have been enormously successful particularly in Brooklyn. Other newcomer criminal gangs pattern their criminal lifestyles after these Rastas and, in a case of imitation being the sincerest form of flattery, newcomer criminals from Panama have mimicked Rastafarian hair locks and dress as a way of breaking into their drug operations.

In Detroit, black gangs, such as the Pony Down and the Young

Boys Inc., have evolved from opportunistic violent street gangs to sophisticated criminal enterprises. Drug dealing is their main business and their membership increasingly attracts middle-class youths as well as the traditional lower-class members. They operate in secrecy, with a small tightly knit core of leaders whose style mimics that of corporate entrepreneurs more than the traditional style of urban street warriors. Their modus operandi suggests that black organized crime is patterning itself after its historical predecessors from the Irish, Jewish, and Italian underworld.

Another section of Brooklyn—Brownsville—illustrates the chronic warfare among American-born and Caribbean-born black gangsters for control of the crack trade. In the late 1980s at least three rival black gangs fought each other for control of this neighborhood. At least eleven murders in a two-year period have been associated with one of these mobs—the Wild Bunch— allegedly headed by Donny Smallwood. Ron Rosenbaum detailed Smallwood's rise to power in a series of *New York Times* articles (February 15, 1987 and November 15, 1987), describing his feuds with "Halfback" James Baker (murdered in 1986) and "Pretty Rob." Whether men like Smallwood can maintain their power over gangs like the Wild Bunch and compete successfully against rival mobs, remains to be seen. Their modes of operation, however, are remarkably similar to those of the Irish, Jews, and Italians of former eras, for a leader like Smallwood "didn't hide his existence in the shadows but boldly made himself a public figure in the community, a provider of parties, dispenser of largess, something like a Tammany Ward boss [corrupt local politician], or an old-fashioned mafia don: a folk hero."

An Unusual Assassination

In another New York City neighborhood, the South Jamaican section of Queens, alleged black criminals, such as "Pop" Freeman, Lorenzo "Fat Cat" Nichols, and Howard "Pappy" Mason have "inherited" the narcotics trade previously operated by the Mafia chieftain, Vito Genovese. Nichols eventually organized the many black competing drug gangs by dividing the territory of that section of Queens among the previously warring factions. . . .

This operation ran reasonably well until Fat Cat's enforcer, "Pappy" Mason, assassinated a New York City police officer, Edward Byrne, in response to an encounter with another police officer who had "dis'ed" (disrespected) him in public. The results of this assassination were disastrous for the entire drug empire of Fat Cat since the entire wrath of the city descended upon his operations. Even the associates of Pappy and Fat Cat were startled and infuriated at such an act which is a clear violation of even the drug dealers' code. One such associate remarked, "Man, I don't know why "Bebo" [Mason] did that. . . . What "Bebo" did was fucked up. He messed up everything for everybody. Now nobody will make no money." Other African American drug dealers quickly occupied the vacuum created by the demise of Fat Cat's operations.

Colombians and Chinese

Colombian gangs are also active in the cocaine traffic; an estimated 75 percent of cocaine consumed annually in the United States is imported from Colombia, supplied by sophisticated gangs that control its importation and processing. . . .

The Colombian gangs often reflect the regional origins of the Colombian newcomers. The so-called Medellin cartel and the Cali cartel derive their names from the two principal cities in Colombia where the cocaine production and distribution are centered. Likewise, the ruthless violence between these two factions has become an everyday occurrence in Miami and New York, where each competes for criminal dominance.

Chinese immigrants form one of the largest segments of Asian newcomers. Historically, Chinese immigrants came from China's Canton province. Current Chinese newcomers come from Hong Kong, Taiwan, Vietnam, Malaysia, and Indonesia, as well as from other sections of China such as Fujian province. Challenging the Cantonese dominance of Chinatown life, these newcomers have formed new gangs that have grown into criminal organizations that control gambling, drug marketing, and that extort money from Chinese merchants. . . .

Like their black and Hispanic counterparts, they are heavily involved in drug traffic, seeking ways to dominate this business within the Chinese community as well as serve as suppliers of "China White" heroin to other gangs and syndicates outside the community. . . .

As America approaches the next millennium, it will witness and record the successes and failures of these new ethnic mobs. Violence and bloodletting will continue; mob czars will emerge, reign, and disappear, replaced by new contenders. African Americans, Hispanics, Asians, and other ethnic newcomers will battle each other in escalating open warfare. Temporary alliances will be made and broken. Politicians, judges, and police will continue to be corrupted as the public maintains its insatiable demand for drugs, gambling, and vice. Prosecutors and press will announce the death of the Italian Mafia only to find new, equally powerful mafias reigning in its place. The cycle of ethnic crime will continue as organized crime supplies the public's demand providing an invaluable opportunity for many newcomers seeking to fulfill the American Dream.

"The skins adopted white supremacist ideologies, from belief in a 'territorial imperative'. . . to the expectation of an Armageddon-like racial holy war."

White Supremacy Fuels Skinhead Violence

David Van Biema

Skinheads espousing white supremacy have beaten or killed minorities in many parts of the United States. In the following viewpoint, David Van Biema explains the separatist ideology that motivates skinhead gangs to beat and kill homosexuals, Jews, and nonwhites. Van Biema contends that although relatively few in number, young skinhead men and women—including young teenagers—are a violent threat to many of America's communities. Van Biema is a senior writer for *Time*, a weekly newsmagazine.

As you read, consider the following questions:

1. What is a "boot party," according to Van Biema?
2. Where does the author trace the source of America's skinhead movement?
3. According to Van Biema, how have white supremacists used skinheads as "front-line troops"?

In a concert grounds in Ulysses, Pennsylvania, down a gravel road off Route 49, on property of a white supremacist named "Chip" Kreis, a weekend-long rock concert is about to begin. A rock concert whose spectators do not appreciate the press. Someone says to a *Time* reporter, "I want to be smiling, I want to get little dimples in my cheeks when I read that article. 'Cause if I don't, I'm going to come and f—ing kill you, do you understand? I'm not f—ing joking, man—look me in the face—I'm going to find you and f—ing kill you." There are hundreds of skinheads gathered here: American Frontists, Confederate Hammerskins, Atlantic City Skins and others from Texas, Colorado, California, North Carolina, Florida, Nebraska, Tennessee and Canada. Their cars, scores of them, are parked around the field; and from the tall antennas wave their banners: in white-and-black, and red, for white supremacists and the neo-Nazis.

At a café a few miles away, the waitress looks haggard. "It started at 5:30 this morning," she says. "Groups of 8 to 12, 14 at one time. And they're talking they want more real estate . . . and we don't want 'em buying more."

Who are the skinheads? For a time it was difficult to divine how many parts monster they were and how many parts fashion victim. The evidence, however, increasingly suggests that they can no longer be perceived merely as exhibits in the great American freak show, good for throwing a chill into Oprah or obliging another host's ego by breaking Geraldo's nose on camera. Rather, the skins have found their niche in American society. It is a far larger niche than most Americans would like them to have, especially as its inhabitants tend to kill people.

According to the New York–based Anti-Defamation League of B'nai B'rith, skinheads have taken 22 victims in the past three years; in 1992 they were responsible for 7 deaths, almost a quarter of all bias-related murders in the U.S. The ADL concluded that the punks, who number about 3,500, are now a bigger racist threat than the Ku Klux Klan. The relatively small death toll, points out Portland, Oregon, police officer Loren Christensen, is misleading. "What makes them real dangerous," he says, "is that it doesn't take many to terrorize a community." Or even a metropolis. Three days after the ADL report, the FBI announced that a group called the Fourth Reich Skinheads had "masterminded" a plot to slaughter the congregation of Los Angeles' First African Methodist Episcopal Church, assassinate well-known black figures around the country and letter-bomb a rabbi.

Skinheads have murdered in every corner of the country. In New York in 1990, 29-year-old Julio Rivera was fatally stabbed and beaten with a hammer by three men connected with the Doc Martens Stompers because he was gay. Later that year in Houston, two skinheads conducted a "boot party" with a 15-

year-old Vietnamese immigrant named Hung Truong. Just before he was stomped to death, according to a detective on the case, Truong pleaded, "Please stop. I'm sorry I ever came to your country. God forgive me." In Salem, Oregon, in September 1992, three members of the American Front group firebombed the apartment of a black lesbian named Hattie Cohens and her roommate, a gay white man named Brian Mock, killing both. And a few months earlier in Birmingham, Alabama, three young skins awakened a homeless black man named Benny Rembert and knifed him to death. It was the killers' idea of celebration; they had been drinking in honor of Hitler's birthday. Says Sergeant W.D. McAnally of the Birmingham police department, who helped arrest several local skins: "Hell, the Klan is a bunch of old farts who ride around shooting and cussing, burn a cross and then go home. These little kids will get worked up and go out and kill somebody."

When the movement peaked in England in the 1970s, "skinhead" was more a punk style statement than a racial stance; "Nazi" skins were just a nasty subgroup, devoted to the bullying of immigrants. Both strains crossed the Atlantic, but in the late '80s, propelled in part by youthful embitterment at the recession economy, the Nazi versions of the skinhead strutted through such cultural crossroads as San Francisco's Haight-Ashbury. They attracted immediate attention for their coiffure, dedication to British Oi! music, black Doc Martens boots and a ferocious appetite for violence—against blacks, gays and Jews. Sometimes the fury turned inward: in August 1987 a California group nailed its ex-leader to a 6-ft. plank. (He survived.) "To be a skinhead," says one participant from those days, "none of the other skinheads are going to respect you unless you go out and mess somebody up, and if you don't, you get messed up."

Such behavior got them on *Oprah* and *Geraldo*. It also captured the attention of onetime Klansman Tom Metzger, head of White Aryan Resistance, California's best-known hate group. Metzger, whose well-developed philosophy includes the expulsion of America's Latinos and Asians and the creation of separatist black and white states, recruited successfully among skinhead groups in the West and Midwest. Too successfully, perhaps. On the last night of a visit by a WAR lieutenant, three Portland, Oregon, skins beat an Ethiopian student named Mulugeta Seraw to death. The case drew national attention, and the Southern Poverty Law Center in Alabama successfully sued Metzger, winning $12.5 million in damages for Seraw's family.

Metzger pulled back—he now calls skinheads "a passing phenomenon" and denies influencing the Fourth Reich Skinheads—but his example heartened other established hate groups such as the Klan, Idaho's Aryan Nations and the Church of the Creator, based in Niceville, Florida. These white supremacists began using skinheads as "front-line troops" in leafletings, recruiting and violent crimes. Says former skin David Mazzella: "The old guys, they were a buncha bench sitters. The skinheads took it to the streets. It was a new resource to rejuvenate these organizations."

Skinhead Teaching

[Jason] was in the skins for two years and got out just before his gang brutally murdered a black man. He initially got into a skinhead gang because he wanted to be tough and associate with others who had a reputation for being tough. "At first," he says, "we didn't hate anyone. We were just a bunch of guys who liked to fight." They would cruise the streets together picking on people of every race, creed, and color.

Then as time went by, Jason's group began to develop a philosophy, the result of meeting a skinhead from an upper-echelon white supremacy organization. The skinhead brought with him a strict set of neo-Nazi, racist beliefs that were accepted by the gang wholeheartedly. Many of the beliefs already existed among some of the gang members, but after they learned a formalized version of white supremacy, Jason and his friends became more ideologically motivated. "We just basically thought as a group," he says.

The experienced skinhead's teaching was the driving force behind how the gang began to act. He was charismatic and somewhat famous for having been on television; the newly recruited skinheads wanted to impress him. "He was a big deal," Jason says. The skinhead teacher would initiate the action, and the student skinheads would roll along with it. Over the next three months, they committed dozens of unprovoked assaults on whites and minorities.

Loren Christensen, *Skinhead Street Gangs*, 1994.

Exposed to such a variety of influences, the skins did what they have always done best—mutated and kept spreading. The movement's accompanying religiosity varies from the Christian Identity's credo about blacks being "mud people" that God made in error on the third day, to Odinism, a worship of the ancient Norse gods. Similarly, the skins adopted white supremacist ideologies, from belief in a "territorial imperative" to be fulfilled by carving out various parts of the continent as all-white enclaves to the expectation of an Armageddon-like racial holy war (often abbreviated to the battle cry "RaHoWa!"). It was RaHoWa that the Fourth Reich Skinheads were allegedly trying to trigger with their assassinations. Explains C.S., a 21-year-old construction worker at the Pennsylvania gathering: "I work with a Dominican guy, and I get along with him better than the white scumbags there, I can tell you that. He knows what my beliefs are—he knows everything." But on Judgment Day, he says, his friend will be wiped out. "He's a decent guy, but when the time comes, that's his problem. If I'm the guy that does the job, that's the way it is. Hopefully I'll be chosen to do the job. Annihilate everyone in our way."

Counter to stereotype, says Danny Welch, director of the SPLC's watchdog group Klanwatch, skinheads include women activists. "Women were in leadership roles from the beginning," he says. "They've been out there with their Doc Martens from the start, stomping people." And while the total skinhead population is small, it is widespread. Locales as divergent as Queens, New York, and Billings (pop. 85,000), Montana, received batches of hate flyers this past year. The town of Hurricane (pop. 3,915), Utah, has its own contingent of skinheads, a group calling itself the Army of Israel, with plans to make the hamlet on the border of Zion National Park a whites-only "homeland."

A new generation, ages 13 and older, is already active, attending boot parties and wearing caps bearing the number 88 (an abbreviation for "Heil Hitler!" based on the fact that H is the eighth letter of the alphabet). Some outgrow the hate; others dress it up. Take Steven McAlpine, 20, a leader of the White Workers Union, which he claims is the fastest-growing skinhead group in the Dallas area. McAlpine has hair. He drives a Mitsubishi and is a political science major at a university in North Texas. He used to belong to a group called the Aryan Defense Force. "It was little young skinheads and stuff," he explains. "As they started maturing and finding out there's more to life than fighting and drinking, as they grew up, they started seeing the political aspects of it, and also the spiritual aspects of it."

McAlpine was a natural for the transition, a political junkie who grew up watching the *MacNeil/Lehrer Newshour* and CNN. His philosophy is the same as ever: a "white sovereign homeland," maybe "all land north of the Rio Grande." "Skinheads grow up," he says simply. "They grow their hair out, they disappear and go into society undetected, and nobody can tell who's who."

More than any of his outrageous colleagues do, he grants an aura of believability to a bit of braggadocio that appeared in the *War Ax*, a "skinzine" published by the Georgia group SS of America:

We are everywhere, and we are nowhere.
You fail to see us, but we are here . . .
We are the predators in your urban jungles.
And our time to strike is fast-approaching.

==

"TV shows depict the rewards of a life of crime and drug dealing."

==

Television May Encourage Gang Crime

Larry Bratt

Larry Bratt is an inmate serving a life sentence for murder at the Maryland State Penitentiary in Baltimore. In the following viewpoint, Bratt contends that inmates at the penitentiary, including young gang members, are watching too many television shows that could encourage future criminal activity. Bratt maintains that shows such as *America's Most Wanted* and *Cops* depict the financial rewards of crime and could teach gang members and others techniques to hone criminal skills and elude police.

As you read, consider the following questions:

1. In Bratt's opinion, what role does television play in prisons?
2. How does Bratt describe the education level of the typical black inmate?
3. According to the author, how do many black inmates view their place in society?

Larry Bratt, "Menace II the Mind," *The Washington Post*, July 11, 1993. Reprinted by permission of the author.

The room is cavernous and filthy, its putrid yellow walls coated with the droppings of the pigeons who, impervious to the wiles of the guards, roam freely throughout the building. You would not think, by the looks of it, that this place would be a haven for hundreds of young, healthy black men. Yet most days every bench and picnic table in this room is filled. For this room houses the large-screen televisions. It is one of the most important places in the Maryland State Penitentiary.

When people outside the world of the maximum security prison imagine life within it, images of rock-breaking labor and backbreaking workouts probably spring to mind. As far as I can see, a more realistic image begins with the theme song of *America's Most Wanted*. As the show blares on the rec area's set, raptness sets in. The inmates are intrigued by what criminal acts others are committing, hoping to pick up possible pointers on how to do whatever crime is being showcased. As importantly, they watch to see if anyone they know—perhaps even themselves—is being profiled.

As the show progresses, all spectators naturally cheer for the fugitive and applaud wildly when one of law enforcement's finest falls by either gunfire or by being outsmarted by the good guy—that is, the criminal. If the outlaw is finally apprehended, the hissing and booing last for minutes. Then, during the commercial break before the next show begins, comes serious discussion on how the criminal could have avoided capture.

I believe there is something wrong with this picture.

A Regular Feature in Prisons

Every day America's four thousand prisons and jails receive an influx of young African American males as new inmates. Many of the million-plus inmates have been convicted of senseless crimes of violence The majority of these young men first encountered crime and a glamorized view of the drug trade through a TV set. Inside—being "corrected"—they now spend the great bulk of their days watching TV.

Having been an eyewitness for the past eleven years, I don't need a newspaper to tell me why this is so. America's prison system is plagued by overcrowding and limited budgets for rehabilitation and counseling. This perhaps explains how TV— low-cost, low-maintenance, wildly popular—has become so central to our lives here. In institutions across America, it has emerged as the pacifier of choice for a population of uneducated and alienated black men. And that fact is not an accident.

In the Maryland penitentiary many of our actions and possessions are severely restricted. Yet every inmate is allowed a television as part of his personal property. In addition the institution provides two televisions in each of the three housing units—the rec area where inmates gather. One TV is for sports and the other for movies and the usual network shows. Besides *America's Most Wanted*, the shows *Cops* and *FBI: The Untold Stories* regularly draw big audiences. On weekends and holidays the institution rents videos that are then shown three times a day. The competing TVs, mingling with the roaring of radios, creates such a cacophony that people in conversation must scream right into the face of the person they are speaking with to be heard.

Eight Hours per Day

When men are locked in their cells they freely watch whatever they want. Between three and four in the afternoon, during the last daytime count to make sure all inmates are still in the institution, a great many men watch the soap operas. Myself included—I'm a *General Hospital* devotee. Afterwards at dinner one can overhear talk about what happened on such and such soap. The bottom line is that practically every inmate in this penitentiary watches television and weekend videos an average of eight hours per day.

This prison society of couch potatoes is a nationwide phenomenon. More than two-thirds of America's prisons are currently wired for cable. In-cell sets are commonplace, and the constant drone of public-area TVs no less than a necessity. This phenomenon is part of an unspoken correctional philosophy. As Donald Cline, associate superintendent at Missouri's Jefferson City Correctional Center, told *Newsweek* in 1992, "I don't want to call it a babysitter, but it's certainly an adult-tender." Unfortunately, it is exactly what the inmates I see here don't need.

Raised on Television

The average age of African American males entering prison today is approximately twenty. The typical inmate has little more than an elementary education. Many do not even know the alphabet. Three-fourths are high school dropouts and an equal number have never held a job for any length of time. Most have grown up in a household without the benefit of male guidance. Is it possible that this lack of education and male supervision has left a void in these young black men? Could it be endless hours of adolescent TV viewing of murders, drug deals and other assorted crimes have simply made these children inured to right or wrong?

Despite confessions by network executives about the consequences of overexposure to TV violence, I'm not so naive as to place TV at the root of all criminal behavior. Yet when I spoke with six newly arrived teenage inmates—all serving life sentences for homicide—they each told the same story. They were raised by a mother who struggled to make ends meet. As children they spent their time going to school, roaming the streets and watching television. They struggled in schools where they felt like outcasts. Unable to relate to a curriculum that did not speak to their experience and their world, ignorant of any skills to make them employable, they sought solace and identity through television.

A Direct Causal Link

The medical community sees a direct link between screen violence and criminal behavior by viewers. In panel discussions on this subject, we usually hear claims from TV and movie industry spokespersons that opinion is divided in the medical community. Different conclusions can be drawn from different studies, so the arguments go, and no clear consensus exists. Yet, the American medical establishment is clear—in print—on the subject of just such a consensus. The American Medical Association, the National Institute of Mental Health, the U.S. Surgeon General's Office, the U.S. Centers for Disease Control and the American Psychological Association have concluded that study after study shows a direct causal link between screen violence and violent criminal behavior.

David S. Barry, *Media & Values*, Summer 1993.

Seeing TV shows depict the rewards of a life of crime and drug dealing as financially profitable, each of these impressionable teens stated that the risks of death or imprisonment were worth it, because they had nothing to live for. So they joined gangs and began dealing drugs for the local drug lords. Today, the general opinion is that when they are released the first thing they are going to do is get a gun. Then they are going to rob so that they can get money. Anyone who gets in their way is going to die.

The Consequences

If TV formed in some large or small way their values upon arrival here, the daily dose of it once inside only furthers that amorality—and adds to it the idea that they are so worthless to society that no effort is being made to educate or train them for something better. Since society considers them not worth saving, they reason, they will continue to treat that society with murderous disdain. . . .

We are a nation known worldwide for our humanitarian efforts. Do we want to be remembered as a people who turned their backs on their own children? Can we allow an entire generation of African American youth to be lost because our officials have concluded that a real effort to reach them would cost a few thousand dollars too much?

And do we really want to suffer the consequences when those young men, gorged on television and starved of all real care, return to the 'hood? Do we really want to discover firsthand that the television culture of America's prisons cannot soothe the savage beast?

"What is driving these young men to become so violent? Well, for one thing, look at the unemployment statistics."

Capitalism Fosters Gang Behavior

Erik Parsels

America's capitalist society has created an environment where gangs and related crime and violence are increasing, Erik Parsels argues in the following viewpoint. Parsels asserts that a lack of jobs and capitalism's win-at-any-cost principle are major reasons that nonwhite males turn to gangs and crime. Parsels is a staff writer for the *New Unionist*, a monthly publication of the socialist New Union political party based in Minneapolis.

As you read, consider the following questions:

1. According to Parsels, what group has been affected most by increased violence?
2. What is the result of a crackdown on crime, in the author's opinion?
3. How are minorities' economic problems a class issue, according to Parsels?

Erik Parsels, "Whipping Up the 'Get-Tough-on-Crime' Hysteria," *The New Unionist*, March 1994. Reprinted with permission.

Just read the newspapers or switch on the evening news. More and more, we seem to be surrounded by a rising tide of violent crime. Our society seems to be breaking down.

To hear the media tell it, hordes of innercity gang members are roaming our neighborhoods, accosting total strangers, or are driving around randomly shooting people. No one knows who will be the next victim.

While this type of sensationalism may boost ratings or sell more newspapers, the idea that the increase in violence is inexplicable, or that the increased risk of harm is shared by all, is a great distortion.

The Facts on Crime

For many of us, the threat of increased danger is more illusory than real. But we continue to be fooled by all the media hype, and we fall right into the waiting arms of our so-called civic leaders, who are pressing for ever-more grim get-tough-on-crime measures.

It is true that violence has increased. It is also true that that same violence is involving more young people than ever before. And it is also true that drug use and gang activity have increased.

It is *not* true, however, that most of the increased violence is gang related. Maybe 5% of killings are. It is *not* true that most people are in significantly greater danger from total strangers. In fact, at least half of all killings are committed by persons who know or are related to the victim. It is *not* true that the increased violence has fallen equally on all parts of society. It has fallen disproportionately on young, nonwhite, working-class males.

Motivating Factors

So what is driving these young men to become so violent? Well, for one thing, look at the unemployment statistics. Those young nonwhite males we just saw in the violent crime statistics also top the unemployment list. That crime follows poverty has never been a secret.

Second, look at the social system we live in. Under capitalism, people are taught that competition is a good thing, that there are two types of people in the world, winners and losers. To be a winner, you have to do whatever it takes to get what you want. If you don't, you're a loser.

The media portrays as heroes [movie characters] like Rambo, who achieve their goals by murder and who have to prove their "manhood" every ten seconds to avoid being called a wimp. For young people whom capitalism has left on the unemployment shelf, these kinds of values can lead to trouble.

Third, take a look at the economics of the situation. Now that corporations have the means to ship jobs overseas, the American worker has watched his and her standard of living deteriorate. Despite the ridiculous and utterly untrue claims of capitalist apologists like Ronald Reagan and Rush Limbaugh that there's a job out there for everyone willing to do an honest day's work, the truth is that capitalism does not and never did provide full employment.

Even the official statistics count only some of those who are out of work. And the statistics completely ignore those who work only part-time and can't earn enough to eat *and* pay the rent. For all his shrill mouthings, has Rush Limbaugh tried living, working and supporting himself at minimum wage? I doubt it.

Drugs and Guns

Without jobs, people in the innercities live impoverished, overcrowded lives. Without steady incomes, the people in poor neighborhoods cannot support businesses, and thereby jobs, in their area. The only "business opportunities" are either drugs or prostitution. These are the only "products" that will bring any money into the neighborhood. As workers, the only other thing that people in poor neighborhoods have to sell is their labor, and no one wants that—there are no jobs.

Youths Are Denied Chances

Within the present class relations of modern technology-driven capitalism, many youths, urban and rural, are being denied the chance to earn a "legitimate" living. An increasing number are white, mostly sons and daughters of coal miners, factory workers or farmers.

Los Angeles, which has more gang violence than any other city, experienced the greatest incidence of gang-related acts during the 1980s and early 1990s, when 300,000 manufacturing jobs were lost in California. According to the Gang Violence Bridging Project of the Edmund G. "Pat" Brown Institute of Public Affairs at California State University, Los Angeles, the areas with the greatest impoverishment and gang growth were those directly linked to industrial flight.

Luis J. Rodriguez, *The Nation*, November 21, 1994.

With the drugs comes the war among the dealers for market share. The fight among the drug dealers and the theft that the jobless addicts resort to to finance their habit frighten urbanites into buying handguns "for protection." These guns are then often stolen or are taken to school by the gun owners' children to show off to their friends. Either way, the guns end up on the streets, in the hands of young people who are at an age where proving your "manhood" in front of your peers is all-important. It is a guaranteed recipe for violence.

But all the get-tough, more-cops-on-the-street, crackdown-on-crime hysteria only makes things worse. By patrolling the streets like an occupying army, the police teach innercity youth that society is their enemy that they should hate. By locking more young offenders up, rather than attack the causes of violence, they help create disturbed, career criminals.

Class and Race Issues

Violence, crime, lack of community values—all these and much more are class-related issues. Capitalism likes to keep a reserve army of unemployed people to help force wages down. That is a *class* issue. They let the burden of that unemployment fall on people of color. That is a *race* issue.

This combination accomplishes two things. It fools nonwhites into thinking that their economic problems are primarily a *race* issue, forced on them by *whites* rather than by *capitalism*. And it forces thousands of nonwhite young men into crime, creating a ready-made bogeyman to terrify the white working class with.

Looked at that way, it is easy to see that the race issue is really a class issue. And it has a long history.

Back before the Civil War, Southern planters made laws to prevent fraternizing between slaves and poor whites, between poor whites and Indians, etc. In the post–Civil War South, whites of all classes were given privileges at the expense of blacks in order to split the working class. If you try to explain this institutionalized racism by saying it's all a personal-hate thing, you'll never get anywhere. Mainly, it was a *class* thing.

Suckered In

The same thing is happening today. For years now, the capitalist media has coordinated its efforts to build up the nonwhite gang member bogeyman. Now, just in time for NAFTA [North American Free Trade Agreement] and GATT [General Agreement on Tariffs and Trade] to facilitate the moving of thousands of jobs to Mexico and elsewhere, everybody has been suckered into supporting this big "get-tough-on-crime" push. When people of color finally rise against their blatant exploitation, the capitalists want to make sure that the white working class doesn't join them.

We saw a dress rehearsal for what may be coming in Los Angeles after the 1992 Rodney King verdict, when L.A. police, having provoked the black community to riot, then stayed off the streets during the riot. This was ostensibly to "avoid further provocation." But the real effect was to allow the TV cameras to get dramatic shots of black and brown looters and the ghastly pictures of blacks beating [white trucker] Reginald Denny.

The effect of these TV pictures was inevitably to lessen the sympathies of white workers for the plight of black workers. By showing minority communities in the worst possible light, the authorities can win the support of white workers for repressive laws that are really aimed as much at them as against black workers.

No Trust in the Ruling Class

So don't buy all the "get-tough" crap. We can never rely on the capitalist-financed and -controlled politicians to solve the problems created by the capitalist system. How can we trust a government that, at the same time it proclaims how much it hates drugs and immorality, finances its banana-republic dictator flunkies by having the CIA fly drugs into our country?

Racism is a class issue. Crime is a class issue. And poverty is certainly a class issue. If we rely on the ruling class to solve the problems that afflict the working class, we can be sure that the "cure" will be worse than the disease.

Periodical Bibliography

The following articles have been selected to supplement the diverse views presented in this chapter.

Elijah Anderson — "The Code of the Streets," *The Atlantic Monthly*, May 1994.

Jordan Bonfante — "Entrepreneurs of Crack," *Time*, February 27, 1995.

Alan C. Brantley and Andrew DiRosa — "Gangs: A National Perspective," *FBI Law Enforcement Bulletin*, January 1995. Available from the Federal Bureau of Investigation, Pennsylvania and Tenth Avenues NW, Washington, DC 20535.

Edward Conlon — "The Pols, the Police, and the Gerry Curls," *The American Spectator*, November 1994.

G. David Curry — "Gang-Related Violence," *Clearinghouse Review*, vol. 28, no. 4, 1994. Available from 205 W. Monroe, 2nd Fl., Chicago, IL 60606-5013.

Donna Hunzeker — "Ganging Up Against Violence," *State Legislatures*, May 1993. Available from 1560 Broadway, Suite 700, Denver, CO 80202.

Robert Hutchinson — "Why Kids Are Ganging Up on America," *Salt*, October 1993. Available from 205 W. Monroe St., Chicago, IL 60606.

Coretta Scott King — "Violent Culture Infects U.S. Teens," *Liberal Opinion Week*, January 17, 1994. Available from PO Box 468, Vinton, IA 52349.

Nathan McCall — "My Rap Against Rap," *The Washington Post*, November 14, 1993. Available from 1150 15th St. NW, Washington, DC 20071.

Deval L. Patrick — "The Rise in Hate Crime," *Vital Speeches of the Day*, October 15, 1994.

Prison Life — "Gangbangers Speak Out: Part 1," March 1995. Available from 505 Eighth Ave., New York, NY 10018.

Tricia Rose — "Rap Music and the Demonization of Young Black Males," *USA Today*, May 1994.

2 CHAPTER

How Serious a Problem Are Gangs?

Chapter Preface

The extent of gang crime and whether it is increasing or decreasing nationally are difficult to measure. For example, the Federal Bureau of Investigation does not categorize youth gang crimes separately, but includes them with other juvenile crimes. On the other hand, according to Donna Hunzeker, a National Council of State Legislatures criminal justice expert, "Where serious crimes have spurred reaction, officials may put many youths and youth crimes under a blanket definition of gangs, comparatively overstating the problem."

Even the opinions of expert gang researchers, though informative, may not clarify the extent of the gang problem. According to University of Southern California sociologist Malcolm Klein, who has studied street gangs for more than thirty years, "There is no doubt about it. Gang membership is increasing, and they are spreading to places other than the large cities." But Klein also maintains, "What gang members do most is nothing. Members typically sleep late, wander around, and gather to watch the action."

Since most gangs do not operate beyond their own communities or metropolitan region, the gang problem is perhaps best measured and addressed on a city-by-city basis. Police in cities such as Tacoma, Washington, have had success ridding streets of gangs, but many officers nationwide fear that some gangs may be too entrenched to eradicate.

The authors of the following viewpoints focus on the seriousness of America's gang problem.

"A second Mafia as large as the first . . . has calamitous implications for the United States."

The Mafia Poses a New Threat to America

Claire Sterling

Claire Sterling has been an American foreign correspondent and investigative reporter based in Italy for more than thirty years. In the following viewpoint, Sterling asserts that the United States is under threat from an influx of Sicilian Mafia gangsters. In America, Sterling contends, the Sicilian Mafia has grown to roughly equal the size of the American Mafia. Sterling argues that Sicilian Mafia members, perhaps more ruthless than their American counterparts, are keeping a low profile in America to avoid the scrutiny of law enforcement.

As you read, consider the following questions:

1. How does Sterling describe the younger successors in the American Mafia?
2. What qualities do Sicilians bring to the American Mafia, in Sterling's opinion?
3. According to the author, which mob bosses were responsible for including Sicilians within the American Mafia?

Excerpted from Claire Sterling, *Thieves' World: The Threat of the New Global Network of Organized Crime*. Copyright ©1994 by Claire H. Sterling Associates, Ltd. Reprinted by permission of Simon & Schuster.

"This is gonna be a Cosa Nostra till I die. Be it an hour from now, or be it tonight, or a hundred years from now, when I'm in jail. It's gonna be Cosa Nostra." [*Cosa Nostra* is a term for the Mafia that means "our thing."] So John Gotti said before a judge sent him up for life. The perceived wisdom today is that he was wrong, but the facts suggest that he may have been right.

Cosa Nostra's end, predicted regularly in America for half a century, *ought* to be near. Over a thousand of its members and associates have been indicted or imprisoned since the 1980s. Its entire governing commission has been convicted. The biological solution awaits its geriatric bosses. Practically all its top patriarchs are behind bars for good anyway, including Gotti himself.

Their younger successors are inexperienced, brash, incautiously greedy, several generations removed from the old mafia culture, and bereft of historical memory. Their discipline is poor. Their humus, the Italian-American community, is washing away into the mainstream of American life. Their hold on the streets seems to be weakening since they lease out rackets to others. Their nerve appears to be slipping, in that they kill less than some of their ceaselessly multiplying and recklessly violent rivals. On the other hand, they are killing each other off more persistently than they have done in decades.

"This is the twilight of the mob. It's not dark yet, but the sun is going down," one expert announced.

Little or No Impact

Yet for the FBI, Cosa Nostra is still "the most serious organized crime problem in the United States." The crime ring that has outlived every other in America since the 1890s is still recruiting, still creaming 20 percent off the top of all new construction in New York, still doing nearly everything it has always done, in the areas that have always been its strongholds.

FBI field officers report that Federal prosecutions have "had little impact on Cosa Nostra's overall activity" in Detroit, "no impact" in Los Angeles, "little effect" in Chicago; that its activities "do not appear to have diminished" in Miami and "remain relatively unchanged" in Kansas City; that the Genovese Family has "a huge operation" in New Jersey where its structure "remains intact."

Nationwide, the organization "remains particularly strong in Chicago, New England, southern Florida, Las Vegas, Atlantic City, and New York City," the FBI says.

"In the universe of organized criminal groups, the racketeering activities of La Cosa Nostra are the most protracted and sustained, the most impacted and entrenched, the most expansive and profitable, the most corrosive and deleterious to legitimate sectors of society, the most resistant to enforcement efforts generally, and the most resilient to the aftermath of any single enforcement effort," observes the FBI's New Jersey office.

The Sicilian Mafia

Second only to this seemingly unsinkable organization is its big brother from Sicily. An independent entity in America since the 1960s, Sicily's Cosa Nostra was supposed to have been finished there halfway through the 1980s when its heroin network was cracked in New York's Pizza Connection case [in which some pizza shops had served as transfer points]. Actually, it has been "growing precipitously," says the head of the FBI's organized crime section, Jim Moody.

It may become a graver menace than its American counterpart, warned Attorney General William Barr in 1992. "I've said this privately, and I've said it at the cabinet table. We are facing a tremendous challenge from the Sicilian Mafia, one that could dwarf La Cosa Nostra here in the United States. We may be at the beginning of a more serious threat from organized crime than ever before," he told a reporter for the *Legal Times*.

There were clear signs by then that the Sicilian Mafia was rapidly colonizing the American underworld. Its men have been arriving legally; visas are no longer required for Italian nationals. Keeping away from big cities inhabited by the American mob and knowledgeable cops, they have been fanning out over the countryside like KGB moles [Soviet spies]. They settle into small towns, file for citizenship, go into business, and win the community's respect. Their names and faces are unknown, and they have no rap sheets in America.

The Sicilian Mafia Grows

The harder the law bears down on the American mafia, the more Sicilian mafiosi arrive. The FBI thought there were a few hundred of them in the late 1980s. By 1991 it was speaking of three thousand, not counting members of the Camorra and 'Ndrangheta [crime rings], "noted with increasing frequency." By the end of 1992 it was estimating "between ten and twenty thousand members and associates." That is roughly the size of the American mafia itself: two thousand members, some twenty thousand associates. A second Mafia as large as the first, accountable to Palermo [capital of Sicily], has calamitous implications for the United States. These are the soldiers formed during [Sicilian Mafia leader] Totò Riina's long and violent reign, veterans of Sicily's Great Mafia War, interlocked with the world's biggest crime syndicates, brutalized to a degree that frightens even their American cousins. They are already drawing the American mafia into their planetary orbit—notably in the sack of Russia—and they can undoubtedly give it lessons in the art of wielding power.

"If you want your Cosa Nostra to be as successful as our Cosa Nostra, you oughtta use Sicilian methods, like killing judges and cops," advised a prize Sicilian trafficker in New York.

Relations between the two mafias have always been mysterious, at times unfathomable. By mutual agreement they have been separate and distinct for some forty years; neither can intrude on the other's sovereign territory. Actually, the Sicilians have occupied several of the Americans' exclusive enclaves since the 1960s and poached all over their criminal preserves.

For the Americans they are the "zips," "geeps," "fuckin' siggies," secretive, predatory, resented, and detested. John Gotti, then the highest boss in the land, had raged against the Sicilians in an exchange with a couple of his soldiers recorded by the FBI:

> FIRST SOLDIER: They're opening up all over the fuckin' place, these zips, ain't they? There's three of them right on this avenue here. They all make money. . . .
>
> SECOND SOLDIER: If they run a game, you know, Johnny [Gotti] will go along with another game. . . .
>
> GOTTI: They're not gonna play nothin'. . . . I got four thousand guys I'll send from every neighborhood, I'll put in there. . . . Let 'em come ahead. Let's see what they'll do.
>
> FIRST SOLDIER: They make like they don't understand, the motherfuckers. . . .
>
> GOTTI: They don't understand what they don't wanna understand. . . . They go around with hundreds of thousands in their pockets, and you're going around with your hat in your hand. . . .

The Sicilian Liaison

Yet the Sicilian Mafia's top emissary to the United States was taken into New York's Gambino Family with "five, six, seven of his crew" in the mid-1970s; a decade later he was elevated to the rank of *capodecina* [regional boss] by John Gotti himself. "You knew then that I made a mistake," Gotti said to his *consigliere* [counselor], Sammy "The Bull" Gravano, who so testified at Gotti's trial in 1992:

> He's discussing the liaison guy from Italy to here who we believe might be a made [initiated] member of our Family and made in Italy and have one foot here and one foot in Italy, and he's doing business.
>
> John Gotti said: "If it's true, if it's him, the liaison guy is getting whacked. . . ." He meant, "If the liaison guy is a made member with us and he has a foot in Italy and he's doing drugs, he's gonna get whacked.". . . The liaison guy is getting whacked because they don't belong to us. That's their crew.

The liaison guy did not get whacked, however. Early in 1987

five different *capos* [bosses] from New York's five mafia Families sat down with him in the back room of the Cafe Giardino, his Brooklyn seat. John Gotti himself drew up in a limousine to call on him soon afterward. From then on he was wintering with Gotti in Florida and seeing him in New York once a week.

The Point Man for Heroin

His name was John Gambino, eldest of the three Gambino brothers of Brooklyn and Cherry Hill, New Jersey, who had come over from Sicily in 1974. Though a distant relative of the late Carlo Gambino, boss of the most powerful Family in America, he answered to the Cupola's [governing body] innermost circle in Palermo.

Arrested in New York on the day that General Manuel Noriega of Panama was arraigned in Miami for collusion with Colombian cocaine cartels, John Gambino received barely a mention in the press. But he had done more than the General to feed America's drug habit.

Tons of heroin had been shipped to him directly in Brooklyn since the 1970s, from Sicilian refineries "transforming and selling heroin to the United States silently, intensively, and continuously," wrote an Italian magistrate. Billions of narcodollars in need of laundering had been entrusted to him, and through him to the Sicilian Mafia's banker in New York, Michele Sindona.

The Mafia's Heroin Trade

The famous French Connection operated between the 1950s and 1970s. Turkish heroin was processed in Marseilles, France, and transported by the Sicilian Mafia to New York and other places in North America.

More recently the Pizza Connection distributed a large share of heroin consumed in the U.S. This loosely affiliated combination of Sicilian and American organized crime families arranged the shipment of heroin to the U.S. and used pizza parlors in the U.S. to shield its heroin operations and related financial transactions.

U.S. Department of Justice, *Drugs, Crime, and the Justice System*, 1992.

In fact, John Gambino could not possibly be whacked, as Gotti discovered when the secrets of Cosa Nostra's previous top boss—the one Gotti got rid of, Paul Castellano—were revealed to him. John Gambino was the diamond point of the whole Sicilian Mafia heroin operation in the United States and guarantor of its longstanding arrangements with the Americans.

The deal, made at a summit meeting in Palermo's Grand Hotel Des Palmes in October 1957, allowed the Americans to divest themselves of the risks in dealing heroin while collecting a share of the profits. The Sicilians took exclusive charge of import and wholesale distribution. The Americans received a rake-off per kilo and announced that they were out of the drug business—officially, right after the Palermo summit, at their historic Appalachian congress in upstate New York.

The Sicilians' Might

Whether or not this was an early sign of the Americans' decline, as some maintain, it marked the beginning of the Sicilians' ascendancy. Once installed in America, they could not be dislodged. Nor, for all their incursions, could they be molested.

They might be feared and disliked, but they were needed—are needed urgently today. American bosses habitually dodge their own ban on drugs by investing money in Sicilian deals. More and more of their soldiers are risking an in-house death sentence to work with Sicilian traffickers. Many Families, running to flab, are in search of more backbone and muscle. For an aging organization tormented by the law and beset by new young rivals, the Sicilians have come to mean fresh blood and the saving strength of ancestral Mafia tradition. Compared to their American cousins, they are still the keepers of the ancient Mafia code, however they may have trashed it. Thus, a growing number of Sicilians "made" at home are getting made in the United States as well. Several have become *capos* in American Families. One has taken over a Family altogether.

Taking the Oath

Spicy evidence to this effect dropped into the lap of FBI agents in Medford, Massachusetts, in the autumn of 1989. Twenty-one members of Boston's Patriarca Family gathered there on a Sunday to induct four new members. An FBI bug picked up every word as a Patriarca captain administered the ritual oath: *"Io, Carmen, voglio entrare in questa organizzazione . . ."*

The oath giver, a Sicilian Man of Honor named Biagio Di-Giacomo, had to explain from time to time in strangled English. "Put your hands out like this, Carmen, and when I read it to you, repeat after me and then go like this, boom, boom, boom," he said, preparing to draw blood from Carmen's trigger finger. He continued:

"If I said you must kill a police informer, would you do that for me on behalf of our organization?"

"Yes, I would."

"You would do that?"

"I would do that."

"This thing of ours, we would be delighted to have you . . ."

Then DiGiacomo continued in Sicilian: "I swear to enter this organization alive and leave it dead." In English, he went on, that meant, "We get in alive in this organization, and the only way we gonna get out is death, no matter what. It's no hope, no Jesus, no Madonna, nobody can help us if we ever give up this secret to anybody. . . . This thing that cannot be exposed. . . ."

The Patriarca Family inducted several more Sicilians in 1992; bugged repeatedly and mercilessly by the FBI, it is plainly in need of their reviving presence. New York's Lucchese Family has sworn in an unregenerate Sicilian drug trafficker, Enzo Napoli. The Philadelphia Family, an exceptionally riotous lot, has actually come under a Sicilian's rule.

Gaining Power in Philadelphia

The Philadelphia Family has dominated crime and politics in much of Pennsylvania for some seventy years, but it started to fly apart when its longtime boss, Angelo Bruno, was shot dead with a sawed-off shotgun in March 1980. A month later Bruno's *consigliere* was tortured, stabbed, and shot to death. A few months afterward his chief loan shark was found stuffed into two green plastic garbage bags. At year's end his successor was blown up by a bomb packed with nails.

The perpetrator, Nicodemo Scarfo, ordered the murders of nineteen more members after he took over—this out of forty in all, replaced by his own men. Ruling with a flamboyance and raw violence much like John Gotti's, Scarfo met much the same end. He was tried for criminal conspiracy and a continuing criminal enterprise—ten homicides, five attempted homicides, extortion, gambling, narcotics—and jailed for life.

The fact that he left the Philadelphia Family in shambles does not altogether explain why the highest echelons of America's Cosa Nostra sent in a Sicilian Man of Honor to replace him. The reputed new boss, John Stanfa, once drove for Angelo Bruno, but he is still a "zip." Born and made in Sicily, he communicates regularly with Palermo's top bosses and is part of their crowd in the United States. Nevertheless, the Gambino Family sent Stanfa down from New York, John Gotti backed him, and Cosa Nostra's national commission even authorized him to swear in a few more Sicilians. Decisions like these are not made casually.

Philadelphia is where the American mafia is "the *second* most serious problem, *after* the Sicilian Mafia," says the FBI. Sicilian drug traffickers infest the city—indeed, they own the whole northern half of it. Angelo Bruno, Sicilian-born himself, turned over the north side long ago to John Gambino and his brothers in nearby Cherry Hill, New Jersey. It is in Philadelphia that the two mafias may decide to remarry after nearly half a century apart: a union of imperial grandeur for the international under-world and a nightmare for American authorities.

The Mafia's Changing Face

There could hardly be much doubt about where such a marriage might lead. "Them fucking zips ain't gonna back up to nobody. . . . Those guys are looking to take over everything. You give them the fucking power . . . they'll bury you. They don't give a fuck. They don't care who's boss. They got no respect," a Bonnano Family captain observed some years ago.

Invited to rejuvenate the American organization, the Sicilians may well end up running it. They will be on their way if they can infuse a once-illustrious American Family with fresh strength.

"A reorganization and perhaps a return to tradition is taking place in the Philadelphia Family and others as well. . . . What is developing may signal a new trend for the organization and operation of La Cosa Nostra," says the authoritative Pennsylvania Crime Commission. "If Stanfa is successful . . . we may see a powerful confederation of Sicilian Mafia members with the remaining Family veterans. Cosa Nostra may emerge as far more powerful, effective, and insulated from law enforcement. The metamorphosis in the Philadelphia Family may represent the future of Cosa Nostra."

This was the attorney general's bad dream: the emergence of a hydra-headed criminal monster in America that would certainly dwarf La Cosa Nostra as we know it.

"The 'Mafia' has come to serve as a mythological belief which excites the imagination [and] entertains the public."

The Mafia Is a Myth

Joseph L. Albini

The Mafia is a myth that was created and sustained by overzealous government investigators and journalists in the 1950s and 1960s, Joseph L. Albini argues in the following viewpoint. Albini contends that sham investigations of the Mafia produced no evidence of the so-called secret society and relied on the questionable testimony of a supposed Mafia figure. Albini maintains that the harmful myth and stereotypes surrounding the Mafia are comparable to those of satanic cults and are equally invalid. Albini is a sociology professor at the University of Nevada in Las Vegas and the author of *The American Mafia*.

As you read, consider the following questions:

1. What was the real motive behind the Kefauver Hearings, according to William Howard Moore, cited by Albini?
2. In the author's opinion, what is the Mafia in Sicily?
3. According to Albini, how did government and the media reinforce each other's belief in the Mafia?

Excerpted from Joseph L. Albini, "The Mafia and the Devil: What They Have in Common," *Journal of Contemporary Criminal Justice*, vol. 9, no. 3 (August 1993). Reprinted with permission.

The Mafia and the Devil, if they are studied and understood from an empirical perspective, are both found to be the creation and product of a belief in a mythological system. Typically, we assume that mythologies are created for and are believed only by children. We fail to acknowledge the fact that mythologies are also created by and for adults. We fail to recognize the fact that mythologies fulfill personal and social needs within the society of which they are a part. We fail, above all, to acknowledge that people will kill or otherwise try to subdue those who are unwilling to agree with or accept their mythological belief. Mythology is power and its belief brings into existence all manner of functionaries that gain and hold social positions entrusted with the responsibility of making certain that the mythology is kept alive and, above all, that the majority of the populace continues to believe in it. . . .

The Creation of the Mafia

Let us turn now to an examination of two current mythological beliefs—The Mafia and The Devil-cults—in an effort to demonstrate how these mythologies were created and what functions they serve in contemporary society. If one examines carefully the conditions and forces that gave birth to the contemporary beliefs in the existence of the "Mafia" and "Devil's Cults," one readily discovers that these were the creations of one or more of the following institutions, agencies, professions or businesses—government investigating committees, law enforcement agencies, journalists and free-lance writers.

The Mafia, as we will show, had its birth in the United States as the invention of the now famous Kefauver Congressional Committee in 1950. Armed with absolutely no understanding of the word, let alone understanding any aspect of its existence in Sicily, Estes Kefauver succeeded in making "Mafia" a terrifying household word. Backed by [bureau head] Harry Anslinger and agents from the Federal Bureau of Narcotics, the Kefauver Hearings produced not one shred of evidence as to the existence of this so-called secret society; but that was not the purpose of the Kefauver hearing. These hearings were meant to be exactly what they were—a great television show. As William Howard Moore (1974) argues, this show was devised in order to draw attention away from the shortcomings and fiascoes of the Harry Truman administration. The show did that; but it did much more. It implanted a symbol in the minds of the American public—the symbol which slowly evolved into a gestalt system of symbols described by Dwight Smith, Jr., as the "Mafia Mystique."

Soon, journalists, armed with Senator Kefauver's production of absolutely no evidence, found a reader's market in which it paid to create more lack of evidence. Ed Reid gave us his bestseller, *Mafia*, which included several paragraphs describing how the "Mafia" began in Sicily. Thousands of papers have been written by scholars still trying to understand all the forces that created Mafia in Sicily, not as a secret society but as part of Sicily's social system; yet Reid managed to condense that history into a few paragraphs.

But here is the first point we must understand about mythological belief—the average person is bored by scholarly writings. So, just a few paragraphs will do. When it comes to building mythological beliefs, it is the conclusion that matters; the facts upon which the conclusion is based are irrelevant.

Along with Reid, *Time*, *Newsweek*, and other magazines were soon featuring stories on the "Mafia" with covers that laid the symbols of what the "Mafia" consists of firmly in the American subconscious mind—hatchets, ropes, chains, knives, machine guns and, above all, a mental and physical profile of what a "Mafioso" looked like. It turns out that he looked very much like an Italian.

Joseph Valachi

But it would not be too long before American television audiences would be shown a real-life Mafioso, Joseph Valachi; he appeared during the McClellan Hearings [on organized crime by the U.S. Senate] in 1963. There was only one problem; Valachi said he had never used the word "Mafia." That did not matter, for the conclusion had already been reached that "Mafia" and Valachi's new term "*Cosa Nostra*" were the same thing. Valachi did not concede that; the President's Task Force did. After all, what did Valachi really know? Evidently, not very much or at least not very much that made any sense to serious students of organized crime. But we must understand that Valachi was not presented to the American public for his knowledge. He was presented to further solidify in the American public's mind a mental picture of the ominous, evil secret society that had taken over America.

If the McClellan investigators had really desired to conduct a valid investigation, they certainly would have questioned the many inconsistencies in Valachi's testimony. Valachi scarcely made one statement without contradicting himself with the next. He told of how powerful the *Cosa Nostra* bosses were and then told about how no one obeyed them. His term, *La Cosa Nostra*, makes no sense in its Italian usage as a term signifying an organization. The words cannot grammatically be used in that manner. But that does not matter. It sounded good. Valachi described a structure of "Boss," "Underboss," "Lieutenant," and "soldier" that was so particularly simple and elusive that it could apply to any organization. Yet the McClellan Committee was so excited about discovering the secret about absolutely nothing. But that is the other powerful ingredient of mythological belief—creating excitement over nothing.

Next, and suddenly, Donald Cressey said that there was something to this nothing. He wrote *Theft of the Nation*, a book that pretended to elevate this simple structure of nothing to a theoretical system worthy of being taken very seriously and above all worthy of serious sociological study. Soon, Italian terms such as "Don" and "Godfather" which were part of legitimate Italian culture were reduced to words that applied only to the "Mafia."

Blaming Sicilians

The current satanic scare is a process of the creation of rumor-panics that often happen in places or locations where there is a great deal of social and economic stress. Like most forms of hysteria, people often feel more safe if they can focus on some cause of their woes. In this case, it is the "Satanic Cults." Similarly, rather than blaming themselves for their desire to use drugs in the 1960s, Americans found it more easy and exciting to blame those foreigners from Sicily who brought the "Mafia" to America and addicted a drug-virgin country.

Joseph L. Albini, *Journal of Contemporary Criminal Justice*, August 1993.

If Cressey had read the works written by anthropologists long before the McClellan Hearings, he would have known that Mafia in Sicily is not and never was a secret society but was and is part of Sicily's historical and social system. As such, it could not be transported to America as the McClellan Committee and Cressey sought to argue. We wonder why Cressey and the McClellan investigators saw "Mafia" as the single-most threat to America when, as Alan Block and William Chambliss point out, the government's own records at the time of the hearings showed that only 16% of those organized criminals convicted between 1953 and 1959 had Italian surnames.

Making Facts Fit

But when one is building mythology one must follow a simple rule: When the facts do not fit, simply force them to fit or completely disregard them. And that is exactly what free-lance writers, journalists and the McClellan investigators did. In a futile effort to try to argue that "*Cosa Nostra*" was a new version of "Mafia," they came up with "purges" in which the "Old Mafia" members all across the United States were killed. No bodies were found. Serious researchers have looked frantically through newspaper obituaries, but not one shred of evidence has turned up. We should have known it was only a story when even the originators of the "purge" story could not give us any names; in fact, they could not even agree on the number that had been killed. What is worse, as Jay Albanese notes, the government and the newspapers and magazines still cannot agree upon how many *Mafiosi* exist today. But they do agree that we should be terrified over the fact that the *Cosa Nostra* is so powerful that it has even corrupted our government. Ironically, while America was watching movies about this menace, our government, through our CIA, was evidently allowing various operators such as Manuel Noriega in Panama and Khun Sa in [Southeast Asia's] Golden Triangle to deal drugs in return for intelligence information. Neither of these traffickers had Italian surnames. And so, the "Mafia" has come to serve as a mythological belief which excites the imagination, entertains the public and draws attention away from real social issues.

Interestingly, the governmental commission reports and the media serve to reinforce each other in creating and sustaining this belief. Thus, (as Thomas Mieczkowski and I have found) when presenting the sources of evidence to support each other's findings, the governmental reports cite the news magazines as their source and the news magazines, in turn, cite the governmental reports. Is there any wonder why they are in total agreement? Is there also any wonder why the large body of serious scholarly researchers who have collected their own data have not been able to find evidence to support a belief in the Mafia? The government investigators argue that these researchers would find the Mafia if they used the government's data, and of course we would, but then we would not be researchers.

Myth Supersedes Reality

And so, while America was being titillated with *Cosa Nostra* stories, our streets and our neighborhoods have become havens for crack houses; daily, citizens, many of them children, are being killed by syndicates battling one another openly in the street. Virtually every ethnic group has become involved. The Colombians, government sources tell us, are responsible for 80% of all cocaine imported into the U.S. But who do we still fear the most—"The Mafia." Why? Because the image of the portrait implanted by mythological belief is far more powerful than reality. That is, unfortunately, the power of mythological belief—it takes on the form of reality.

And so, joining in the Mafia in this world of mythological distortion, we now have the current hysteria of "Devil's Cult.". . .

Historically, we know that witches (those people who, as the belief goes, sold their souls to the Devil in order to receive power) were discovered and put to death. The Salem Witch Trials and the Inquisition are the best examples. But we should not be surprised that governmental tribunals entrusted to find witches always do. Why? Because they are the ones that decide what characteristics witches possess. Once decided and accused, if a witch denies being a witch when interrogated, that, in itself, is absolute proof that he or she is a witch. We now see the power of those investigating bodies intrusted with the ability to label. In this respect, we recall Senator Kefauver's reactions to those Italians called before his committee and asked the question: "Are you a member of the Mafia?" If they replied "No," Kefauver and the committee said that this was definite proof that they were of the Mafia. And so, neither those branded as witches nor those labeled *Mafiosi* had a chance. To be accused, in itself, is to be convicted.

As we look at the current hysteria concerning "Devil's Cults," we find that, like the "Mafia," it is the creation of journalists who want to excite the public but do so with unfounded facts and the creation of certain types of law enforcement agents, now called "Cult-Cops.". . .

Among the crimes that the "Cult-Cops" are reporting, are serious mutilations of animals employed in the satanic rites; the brutal killing of newborn babies to obtain sacred blood in order to enhance their powers; the desecration of cemeteries in order to obtain bones and other body parts; the sexual abuse of children to pay homage to the Devil; forcing women to dance nude and have sex with the members of the group and a host of other bizarre behaviors.

Are these crimes in fact happening? According to the "Cult-Cops" and the believing public, they are. According to law enforcement statistics as reflected in indictments, they are not.

Total Absurdity

Here again, as in the case of creating the Mafia, we see the journalists at work. A best-selling book, *Cults that Kill* by Larry Kahaner, is a perfect example. The book consists of report after report by "Cult-Cops," professed satanists and various authorities on cults. The ad on the cover reads: "This book is a shocker." In my opinion, the only thing that is shocking is that, after all the presentation of gory details, there is no indication that any of these crimes ever occurred or resulted in an indictment. All there is in such books consists of so-called "facts" presented in such a way as to give the reader the creeps. Just as journalists in the 1960s were trying to convince Americans that the Mafia had control of America, these journalists today are trying to tell us that we should not venture outdoors because the Devil's disciples are waiting to grab us and turn us into something to eat for their evening meal. This is a total absurdity—but it sells books.

It also raises the status of the police detectives who go looking for these satanists. As Larry Hartsfield observes, in America, historically and socially, the role and status of the detective have been mutually tied to those of the professional criminal. As a detective, one gets more points for chasing clever criminals as compared to ordinary ones. Thus in the 1960s, those detectives who were "Mafia-Hunters" won status for dealing with the supposedly clever criminal mind of a *Mafioso*. Today's "Cult-Cops" get points for doing battle with the "evil mind" of the satanist. Yet neither the "Mafia-Hunters" nor the "Cult-Cops" realize that they are fighting a creature of their own mental creation and their overworked imagination. . . .

Harmful Mythologies

And so the "Mafia" and "Satanic Cults" turn out to be mythologies. But they are harmful ones. I personally know of too many stories of honest, law-abiding Italians who in the 1960s could not obtain jobs or lost their jobs because their employers thought they belonged to "the Mafia."

I know of a mother who watched in horror as her house burned down, knowing that her newborn baby was inside it and could not be rescued. That was traumatic in itself. More traumatic, however, was her arrest when police found among the ruins a book on Magic. They suspected she had killed her child as part of a satanic ritual. Fortunately, her lawyer was able to talk sense into the police and she was released.

So, in conclusion, the Mafia and the Devil-cults are the creations of journalists with overactive imaginations, governmental investigation committees that are basically self-serving, law enforcement officers with a religious fervor and a fear of their own making. They originate from facts that either do not exist or are based upon profound exaggeration and serve as scapegoats for an American public that cannot face itself for what it is. These are what the "Mafia" and the "Devil's Cults" have in common.

"Street gangs are not loosely formed groups of individuals. In many instances, they have become informally structured business enterprises."

Street Gangs Are Dangerous Criminal Enterprises

D. Saccente

D. Saccente is a retired police investigator with the state of Connecticut's Asset Forfeiture Unit. In the following viewpoint, Saccente argues that street gangs must be considered and targeted as organized criminal enterprises. Saccente maintains that street gangs—using violence and committing crimes for profit to finance the preservation of their organizations—are structured similarly to organized crime families. He cites the broad scope of racketeering and forfeiture laws as an effective way to convict gang members and seize their criminal assets. Saccente is now a senior investigator with an Enfield, Connecticut, insurance firm.

As you read, consider the following questions:

1. What is the purpose of racketeering laws, according to Saccente?
2. What does the author identify as crimes committed by street gangs for profit?
3. According to Saccente, what investigative tools can law enforcement use to enforce racketeering laws against gangs?

The criminal activities of street gangs affect all citizens throughout the United States. Crime statistics show that these street gangs are involved in crimes such as drug trafficking, fraud, robbery, assault, larceny and murder. Their activities are not localized, but span cities, towns and, in some cases, states. The jurisdictional lines of law enforcement create obstacles that hinder the investigation of the continuing criminal activities. The impact of the criminal gangs is felt far beyond the city limits, but these same city limits are the roadblocks that force law enforcement agencies to seek other avenues of investigation. Unless a broad investigative approach is implemented to break through the invisible barriers that offer protection to the organization, these gangs will continue to function despite the continuing arrest and prosecution of their members.

The objectives in the investigation of street gang criminal activity are to identify, arrest and successfully prosecute the gang members and ultimately dismantle the gang itself. In many cases, however, an arrest of one member of the gang is treated as an isolated incident. Little attention is paid to the organization's overall activities. An effort must be made to attack the gang as a whole.

Federal and state racketeering laws, along with asset forfeiture laws, provide the means to overcome these barriers, since these laws have no boundaries. They permit the seizure of profits realized from the criminal activity of these gangs. RICO (Racketeering Influenced and Corrupt Organization) laws deal with the criminal activity of the organization, while asset forfeiture laws deal with the assets obtained from the activity.

Laws Against Criminal Enterprises

To begin using these laws effectively, law enforcement agencies must first view street gangs as criminal organizations. Street gangs are not loosely formed groups of individuals. In many instances, they have become informally structured business enterprises.

Racketeering prosecutions are commonly applied to corporate structures, political corruption, organized crime and violent activist groups. A closer examination of racketeering statutes throughout the United States reveals that these laws—designed to provide a powerful tool in combating crime—also deal with other types of criminal enterprises.

Since there are broad interpretations of "who" or "what" can be prosecuted under RICO statutes, the police must look at what their laws define as an enterprise. Connecticut's Corrupt Organizations and Racketeering Activities (CORA) Act, for example, defines an enterprise as "a sole proprietorship, individual, corporation, business trust, union chartered under the laws of the state or other legal entity or any unchartered union, association or group of individuals, associated in fact although not a legal entity."

Crips Franchising

Quintin Stephen was often in Denver to do business. Back in Los Angeles, he ran Nu U Productions, a recording studio whose stable included several rap acts. But the 6-ft.-tall, conservatively dressed Angeleno was not in Colorado to sell music. He was there as "Q," the name he went by on the streets of Los Angeles, where police and the FBI say he belonged to the Eight Trey Gangster Crips. Q was out to expand his criminal franchise. . . .

Before long he had expanded to five other cities, as far east as Birmingham, Alabama, and Atlanta. It was a cross-country advance that was halted only by an intense investigation coordinated by the FBI over five states, which included the arrest in February 1995 of a fugitive who had been on the run since September 1993. The so-called Eight Trey Gangster Crips network is estimated to have distributed hundreds of kilos of crack and cocaine powder worth well in excess of $10 million on the street. And Q's network, according to the FBI, is only one of perhaps a hundred more in operation. They emanate from Los Angeles' increasingly expansionist gangland. Says FBI special agent-in-charge Charley Parsons in Los Angeles: "The gangs are literally franchising themselves."

The story of businessman Q, as reconstructed from police and court records, traces a prodigious feat of colonization and franchising. In Los Angeles, Q and his cohorts made their basic profits from cocaine bought at cross-border prices—typically about $15,000 a kilo. They cut the coke and ratcheted up the price as they resold supplies in outlying markets. Then with expansion came branches and outposts beyond the bounds of Los Angeles, as well as franchise-like agreements with local, allegedly gang-connected distributors.

Jordan Bonfante, *Time*, February 27, 1995.

The principal phrases in this definition—"individual," "association" and "group of individuals"—deserve close scrutiny. Most street gangs' organizational structure consists of a group of individuals. Police departments have routinely identified the rank, status, position and roles of the members within the hierarchy. Although informal, the structure resembles that of organized crime families. Usually the leaders do not actually participate in the gang's criminal activities; instead, these activities are carried out by lower-ranked members. The loyalty of the members can be compared to that of a family. In many cases, the gang has geographical boundaries and its members are from the same ethnic background. The profits gained from the illegal activities are used to finance the preservation and continuing operation of the gang.

Street gangs are known to use violence, fraud, intimidation and murder to enforce and protect their enterprises. Their criminal activity includes crimes such as larceny, robbery, burglary, credit card fraud, receiving and/or selling stolen goods, narcotics distribution and arson. They prosper as a result of these "crimes for profit."

Since these gangs accumulate large sums of money, they must utilize legitimate businesses, financial institutions, family members, lawyers and other professions to process and hide their assets. An overview of the gang problem shows that, like organized crime, their activities affect almost every aspect of society.

The Connecticut CORA statute provides the following definition of "racketeering activity": ". . . to commit, attempt to commit, to conspire to commit, or aid, solicit, coerce or intimidate another person to commit any crime which, at the time, was a felony" under statutes such as gambling, homicide, assault, prostitution, kidnapping, burglary, arson, larceny, robbery, forgery, drugs and firearms. CORA further defines a "pattern of racketeering activity" as "engaging in at least two incidents of racketeering activity that have the same or similar purposes, results, participants, victims or methods of commission, or are otherwise interrelated by distinguishing characteristics including a nexus to the same enterprise." Each incident must be a separate occurrence and not be additional inclusive charges for one action.

Penalties and Prosecution

The penalty for CORA in Connecticut is imprisonment for a definite term of not less than 1 year nor more than 20 years, or a fine of not more than $25,000, or both. Additionally, anyone found guilty of CORA violations shall forfeit any property that has been acquired, maintained or used in violation of CORA, including profits, appreciated value thereof or proceeds from the sale thereof; and any interest in security of, claim against, or property or contractual right of any kind affording a source of influence over any enterprise that he has established, operated, controlled, conducted or participated in the conduct of, in violation of this law.

Violation of CORA is prosecuted as a separate crime, in addition to the charges related to the racketeering activity. For example, if an individual is charged with several predicate acts (such as the sale of narcotics), he would be prosecuted for those charges. If he is found guilty and sentenced, he would then be prosecuted for CORA and be subject to the imposition of an additional sentence or fine.

Connecticut's CORA statute provides a formula for use in determining whether or not a CORA investigation should be initiated: *person + enterprise + two predicate acts = CORA*. Typically, the main problem in any racketeering case is identifying the "enterprise." In the case of street gangs, however, law enforcement officials and members of the gang have made such identification easy.

The intent of this racketeering statute is not only to arrest the individuals involved in the enterprise but to remove the assets gained or used to maintain the enterprise. Since many of the crimes committed by members of the gang are motivated by greed, removing the profits will make a major impact on the gang's structure and strength.

Law enforcement officers should seriously consider targeting street gangs as enterprises. In most cases, the leader and structure have been identified, and the predicate acts are usually part of the criminal histories of both leaders and members. Court records and criminal histories, supplemented with prosecutorial assistance, could lead to the arrest of members, and subsequent dissolution of the gang. . . .

Investigative Efforts

Since there are forfeiture provisions set forth in most racketeering statutes, the investigation should be directed toward financial disclosure of the gang, its members and the members' families. Many departments have asset forfeiture officers and/or financial analysts who are experienced in the financial investigative effort; such people are a valuable resource in these investigations.

Of course, research into the criminal histories of gang members must also be conducted. Police reports and intelligence records must be gathered and shared by police departments. Analysts must try to diagram the gang's structure and identify the members and their positions and roles. An initial diagram may change regularly as more information is gathered, but you must begin somewhere.

Financial investigators must research public, financial and business records, and—in some cases—vital statistics such as birth, marriage, divorce and death records to disclose assets. Investigative tools such as search warrants, subpoenas, wire taps and grand jury inquiries should be considered, since they will help produce evidence not only of crimes committed but of the enterprise's existence and assets.

The overall investigative effort must address the entire gang organization and its auxiliary components, such as businesses and professional assistance. In many cases, police will identify not only members of the gangs, but legitimate businesses used to launder money—professional people such as lawyers and businesspeople who aid the continuing operation and existence of the gang.

Many states have organized gang task forces in efforts to eliminate their violent and criminal activities. Modern police technology and investigative techniques have assisted in the successful investigation and prosecution of a number of street gang members. Legislatures have passed racketeering laws with strong sanctions and penalties. The police, the criminal justice system and the judiciary must work together to accomplish the common goal of breaking the structure of street gangs.

RICO, money-laundering and asset forfeiture laws, although different, have a common thread: they complement each other in their efforts to arrest and prosecute gang members and ultimately weaken the street gang structure.

"[A] perception of gangs as an alien presence or an invading force dominates high-profile news accounts even in the face of contradictory evidence."

Many Street Gangs Are Not Dangerous Criminal Enterprises

Jeffrey J. Mayer

Street gangs may not be as criminally oriented or well organized as they are often perceived, Jeffrey J. Mayer argues in the following viewpoint. Mayer contends that many journalists, prosecutors, and others tend to incorrectly label all street gangs as tight-knit criminal enterprises. But inner-city youths and others associate for a variety of reasons unrelated to crime, Mayer asserts. Mayer is an attorney for the law firm of Raymond and Prokop in Birmingham, Michigan.

As you read, consider the following questions:

1. What role does pleasure play in gang activity, according to Mayer?
2. Why is youths' adoption of gang symbols not necessarily related to crime or gang membership, according to Mayer?
3. What misconceptions does the author note in a Department of Justice description of Operation "Weed and Seed"?

From Jeffrey J. Mayer, "Individual Moral Responsibility and the Criminalization of Youth Gangs," *Wake Forest Law Review*, vol. 28, no. 4 (Winter 1993), pages 943-86. Reprinted with permission.

The gang debate lacks an adequate understanding of the subject. Prosecutors, legislators, columnists, and academics uniformly side-step the definition of a "gang" when proposing or devising anti-gang strategies. Observers treat gangs in different ways, but rarely distinguish among different types of gang organizations. The primary consensus is that a gang is a group with social, racial, or ethnic ties that acts to further a criminal purpose. Indeed, if an organization lacked either social ties or a criminal purpose, it would not be the type of organization giving rise to anti-gang hysteria. The two dominant theories of gang organizations link these two characteristics in radically different ways. One school views gangs as primarily social units, while the other considers a gang's presumed criminal purpose as the organizing principle. . . .

The media treats gangs and their presence or absence in a community as a fact apart from the people of the local community, something akin to a disease or a military attack. This perception of gangs as an alien presence or an invading force dominates high profile news accounts even in the face of contradictory evidence.

Shortly after the Los Angeles riots, the *New York Times* described a truce between "the city's rival gangs, the Crips and the Bloods," in an article entitled "Hope and Fear in Los Angeles as Deadly Gangs Call Truce." The *New York Times* further reported that "[many] people around Los Angeles are surprised to see signs of accord between the two dangerous gangs, *whose members have been sworn enemies for more than two decades*" [emphasis added]. The article continued to describe the "two gangs" as powerful nationwide enterprises. . . .

False Images

Yet, the *New York Times'* depiction of the "two gangs" as monolithic armies of terror is contradicted by the article itself. The reporter acknowledged that "[t]he gangs are not tightly structured, hierarchical organizations, but loose confederates of small neighborhood gangs." Consequently, the reporter's description of the gangs as eternally feuding, hierarchical organizations is simply not true, but nonetheless perpetuates the image of gangs as organizations in which social ties, criminal purpose, and outward indicia of gang membership necessarily overlap. . . .

In *The Drug Wars: An Oral History from the Trenches*, Tim Wells and William Triplett interviewed teenagers and young adults involved in the use and sale of illegal narcotics. The dealers generally operated alone and were only loosely allied with other drug traffickers. One youth stated, "I come to Miami from Cuba. I didn't have no family, and I starting fucking around. . . . I start selling drugs." Another noted, "I used to work for this guy that had one of the biggest cocaine distribution networks in the city."

Both youths were small players in the larger scheme and did not form criminal alliances with their friends or neighbors. One joined "with a group of Puerto Rican guys, the Puerto Rican Mafia." The other worked "for this guy that had one of the biggest cocaine distribution networks in the city. . . . He had an L.A. connection, some people there that had access to cocaine coming into the U.S. from Colombia." Neither operated as part of a gang, nor was the larger organization a youth gang. Instead, the bigger drug trafficking organizations were adult criminal conspiracies, perhaps organized along ethnic lines, but devoted to making money through large scale criminal enterprises, not the street violence associated with youth gangs.

Seeking Pleasure

Youth activities, whether criminal or otherwise, are also about pleasure. If the motivation for joining a gang is pleasure and not criminal gain, social ties and criminal purpose also diverge. In such cases, criminal purpose may form a part of the youth organization's concerted efforts. For example, many gang members, when interviewed, referred to the enjoyment they received from participation in gang activities, some of which were criminal. The pleasure may be difficult to comprehend, but the image of the gang member as an angry criminal is often inaccurate. Not only is the criminal activity often secondary to the pleasures of friendship, but also the criminal activity itself is often carried out for pleasure, not criminal gain. The fact that pleasure manifests itself as crime is simply a brutal and disheartening truth. While some social activities may also be criminal, common pursuit of pleasure is not synonymous with a unifying criminal purpose.

Gang Identity and Symbols

Gang identity and criminal purpose also diverge. The outward symbols of gang identity often mask unconnected units or are adopted for reasons of self-preservation or fashion. The appearance of a new gang is, according to Alex Kotlowitz, often the work of "wannabes" or "pee wees" not involved with criminal activity.

> Frequently, young boys at Horner [a Chicago public housing project] claimed allegiance to one gang or another. *Children as young as four or five at a neighborhood preschool program would arrive each day with their hats turned to the left, showing allegiance to the Vice Lords, or to the right, for the Disciples* [emphasis added]. A group [of pre-teenagers] like the Four Corners imitated their older counterparts. But there was no real organization or discipline; moreover, they didn't sell drugs.

Gang association, except for the "wannabe" or "pee wee" aspiring members, may stem from a variety of motives. Outward manifestation of gang identity, notably particular clothes and signals, may indicate luxury or power in a particular neighborhood. Certain social behavior, such as associations with gang members and knowledge of gang signs, also may be a matter of survival. Young males may have to make peace with local gangs to go to school, work, or merely walk around the neighborhood. In other circumstances, markers of gang activity blend with the traits of young minorities.

Disorganization

Street gangs are said to be well-suited to drug distribution because of their internal structure, which is hierarchical and highly controlled. In fact, however, street gangs are normally loosely structured and ill-controlled. Turnover is heavy and relatively constant, so that experienced members wax and wane in their participation, while older members are rapidly replaced by new recruits. Only in *West Side Story* is control wielded effectively by the few: in real street gangs, multiple cliques, dyads, and triads are the common units of companionship, each responsive to its own age peers rather than to powerful (or older) leaders. For drug distributors, such a haphazard organizational structure does not provide the basis for an effective distributional system.

Malcolm W. Klein and Cheryl L. Maxson, *Drugs and Cocaine*, 1994.

The divergence between gang symbols and criminal purpose also extends to the apparent national scope of certain gangs. The image of the street gang on the move dominates many news accounts. As [an] Atlanta housewife said, "[the gangs] are beginning to stretch out." In fact, gang symbols frequently move independently of the gangs. As youths copy gangs in other cities, gang symbols often indicate little more than gang publicity. For example, according to the U.S. Department of Justice, a Kansas City police profile of local gangs acknowledged that the links between Kansas City and Los Angeles gangs are purely superficial: "Kansas City gang members attempt to emulate Los Angeles gang members, but the locals are still learning the gang style. It is apparent in their style of clothing, mannerism, language, and graffiti. They are still wannabes."

At the same time, young criminals branch out to different locations without the benefit of an intricate gang structure. "Fast Freddie," a drug dealer, explained:

In New York and Washington, D.C. the crack scene is very competitive. There are lots of people selling on the streets. So what I decided to do was branch out into the western states— Utah, Idaho, and Wyoming. I have some friends out there and they said they could move it. So I got in my van and drove a kilo out to Utah.

Thus, street gangs are not franchises distributed by clever inner-city youths to expand criminal activity. Rather, the spread of gang symbols and criminal behavior occurs independently.

A related problem of equating gang identification and uniform criminal purpose is the constant emergence of new splinter gangs and gang symbols. Are the Grape Street Watts a Crip set and related to the Warrior Grape Street Watts, and are the Warrior Grape Street Watts also a Crip set? If the Bounty Hunters are a Blood set and enemies of the Crips, are they also enemies of the "Block Bishops"? Are the Hoover Crips and Outlaw Crips affiliated? And what is their relationship with the Rollin' Sixties? These questions cannot be easily answered. Thus, even when youths consciously adopt gang symbols, they are not necessarily criminals or even gang members.

Black and Chinese "Street Gangs"

Examples of gang activity certainly do not prove that no street gang constitutes a social unit with a criminal purpose, identifiable through gang symbols. However, in many prominent prosecutions of purported street gangs, the criminal organization was not the type of street gang now triggering the massive anti-gang efforts. The [black] El Rukns of Chicago are often called a street gang and cited as a symbol of the gang problem. The El Rukns, however, have many members over thirty and are led by Jeff Fort, a federal prisoner over forty years old. Although some El Rukns met as youth gang members, recent El Rukn crimes are not youth gang crimes.

Similarly, New York appears to host several competing criminal organizations involving Chinese-Americans. Gangs such as the "Green Dragons," the "Ghost Shadows," and the "Flying Dragons" have their own traditions and are organized along ethnic lines. These gangs, writes Frederick Danner in a 1992 *New Yorker* article,

> have a distinctive culture—a bizarre mixture of traits borrowed from the Hong Kong triads (secret criminal societies) and the cliches of American and Chinese gangster movies. Gang members dress all in black and have their chests and arms tattooed with dragons, serpents, tigers, and sharp-taloned eagles. They can be as young as thirteen.

The Chinese "gangs" are not involved in street level drug trafficking, but engage "in a recognizable pattern of racketeering, the bedrock crime being extortion." The Chinese gangs do not perpetrate the violent street crime indicative of the society-wide moral breakdown which requires a massive response. The Chinese gangs also do not cause mass terror on the streets of New York, even though these gangs fit the standard assumptions regarding the convergence of social identity and criminal purpose.

Inadequate Definitions

Given the diversity of gang structures, the construction of an adequate working model for youth gang prosecution is understandably difficult. Even law enforcement agencies acknowledge that youth gangs are not subject to a standard definition. However, the prosecution of youth gangs as entities must begin with some understanding of youth gangs. Recent law enforcement efforts to address street gang crime, therefore, have attempted to define what constitutes a youth gang. These efforts draw partially from the pervasive, yet clumsy, false objectivity of correctional criminology. Consequently, officials attempt to structure prosecutorial measures on an inadequate definition of youth gangs. Thus, the efforts are severely handicapped.

The difficulty with the law enforcement definitions, however, goes far beyond a difference in opinion between law enforcement officials and social scientists. Criminal conspiracies take innumerable forms and cannot be categorized with one or two standard templates. Any attempt to create such a template results in a model that is either overly broad or excessively narrow. Notwithstanding the lack of data and difficult racial issues, officials have defined gangs as organizations sharing social ties, a criminal purpose, and gang indicia. Other officials appear to have assumed a commonly accepted definition. For example, a 1989 Department of Justice publication began with the ubiquitously ominous rhetoric of moral breakdown: "Youth gangs and their illegal activities are continuing to escalate around the Nation despite intensive efforts by law enforcement and prosecutors to curb them, according to experts who addressed a national youth gang conference in Los Angeles." After this introduction, the authors do not attempt to explain what a gang is, what a youth gang is, or how to identify gang members.

Wrong Assumptions

Similarly, a 1992 description of the much-heralded Department of Justice program *Operation "Weed and Seed"* is no more helpful, stating only that it "is a community-based, comprehensive, multi-agency approach to combatting violent crime, drug use and gang activity in high-crime neighborhoods." Inherent in the Department of Justice statement is the belief that the term "gang activity" is as self-explanatory as "violent crime." Furthermore, the Department assumes that gangs, when identified, have at their core a criminal purpose.

Prosecutors, police, legislators, and academics have internalized the popular assumptions regarding youth gangs and incorporated them in the anti-gang efforts. While the definitions of gangs offered by the experts often differ in complexity and style, they uniformly fail because they assume that ethnic gangs invariably have a criminal purpose. If the definitions and subsequent law enforcement measures rely upon social markers to identify juvenile criminals, their scope is overly expansive and open to abusive application against minority teenagers. However, if the anti-gang efforts omit mention of the social characteristics of gangs, the efforts remain open to abuse and, more importantly, are reduced to pointless restatements of standard conspiracy law. The ultimate failure of all these definitions lies in the fact that the entity sought simply does not exist. . . .

[A 1991 Department of Justice] report concluded that gangs should be attacked even if they cannot be classified as an organization. The report noted that "whatever type of gang may be present, the fact that there is a gang, *however loosely knit* [emphasis added], has great tactical significance. When gangs act on a recurring basis, their interests become clearer, their criminal activity more predictable, their vulnerability to detection greater."

The Significance of Individuals and Membership

The assertion of universal gang criminality is undermined by the substance of the report itself. Although the report proposed a number of anti-crime strategies, it confidently asserted that in San Diego "[t]he most effective targeting technique consisted of gaining specific information on offenders from beat officers." The report further stated that "[a]nother effective technique involved using confidential informants (CIs) to identify target offenders. These CIs were used for the sole purpose of determining which members of a particular gang should be targeted." The emphasis on individual offenders weakens the preceding claim that a gang operation, no matter how loosely knit, is of great tactical significance.

The Justice Department report presented data that gang membership and gang violence were unrelated: "It appears that there has been a positive impact on the level of gang violence in San Diego. *Although the police department reports gang membership up [thirty-one] percent in 1990 compared to 1989, they report [a fifty percent reduction in gang-related homicide] for the same period"* [emphasis added]. If gang membership itself was meaningful, a thirty-one percent increase in gang membership could not be reconciled with a fifty percent drop in gang-related homicide. The report thus evidences a struggle to maintain the established understanding of gangs as an alien and immoral presence. The temptation to develop a conceptual construct based upon social stereotypes makes it difficult to focus on the reality of gangs as groups of individuals.

*"The intimidation of witnesses, and their
subsequent killing, is on the rise, especially in
gang-related crimes."*

Gang Intimidation
of Witnesses Is a
Growing Problem

Sam Howe Verhovek

Many witnesses to gang crimes are reluctant to testify against
gang members for fear of retaliation. In the following viewpoint, Sam Howe Verhovek describes the tactics gang members
use to intimidate witnesses. Verhovek contends that such intimidation, including murder, is increasing and that gang members
are routinely pressuring witnesses not to testify against them.
Verhovek is the *New York Times* bureau chief in Houston, Texas.

As you read, consider the following questions:

1. In Kerry Murphy Healey's opinion, cited by Verhovek, why
   may some witnesses be reluctant to get involved in crime
   cases in poor urban areas?
2. How have some cities sought to protect the safety of
   witnesses, according to Verhovek?
3. According to the author, why have Los Angeles prosecutors
   videotaped trial spectators?

Three months after his testimony helped convict a gang member of murder, and just one week before he was to testify in the trial of a second defendant, 19-year-old Elijah Ragland was found dead in a creek in east Fort Worth, Texas.

He had been repeatedly shot in the head and neck. And though the killing in January remains unsolved, the police say they believe it was related to Mr. Ragland's testimony.

The police and family members say Mr. Ragland had received several threats warning him to stay away from the second trial. But Mr. Ragland was willing to do what an increasing number of witnesses to crimes are not: testify in court.

Prosecutors around the nation say the intimidation of witnesses, and their subsequent killing, is on the rise, especially in gang-related crimes. People who provide investigators with detailed information about crimes are refusing to divulge the same information in a trial at which they must publicly face the accused.

In testimony before a Congressional committee, prosecutors in Washington said the city was failing to pursue 30 percent to 35 percent of its murder cases because people with knowledge of events refused to cooperate.

Gang Threats

There are few other reliable statistics on witness intimidation. But the anecdotal evidence is powerful. . . .

In Oakland, California, the police have reported several cases in which witnesses at upcoming trials for gang-related killings have had their pagers go off, flashing what turns out to be the number of a local mortuary.

In Los Angeles, prosecutors say that gang members will sit as spectators at a compatriot's trial, slowly moving an index finger across their throats in a slashing motion as a witness is taking the stand.

Barbara Thompson, a spokeswoman for the Manhattan District Attorney's office, said witness intimidation had a profound effect on prosecution in New York. "We feel that there is probably a hidden world of witnesses who never come forward," she said.

And if the witnesses are compelled to testify, they are often a fiasco on the stand—"going sideways," is what the police and prosecutors call it—saying they do not remember details of the incident or offering an account that would exonerate the defendant.

It can destroy a case. "You're frustrated, you're so frustrated," said Terri Moore, the former chief prosecutor in the gang unit of the District Attorney's office in Fort Worth, who has watched solid cases collapse when witnesses have lost their memories on the stand.

"The worse the criminal is, the more likely the witnesses are to be intimidated," Ms. Moore said. "So you have the most heinous of criminals about to walk free because these people are so terrified. This is supposed to be about justice, and sometimes you have to just stand there while evil seems to prevail."

So compelling are the anecdotes that the Justice Department has commissioned a major study of witness intimidation.

Witnesses at Risk

Kerry Murphy Healey, a consultant with Abt Associates Inc., the social policy research concern in Cambridge, Massachusetts, that conducted the study, said witness intimidation was most severe in poor urban neighborhoods, where shootings often occur in broad daylight and many witnesses know the killers.

"A lot of these killings are perceived as being private business matters," Dr. Healey said. "Witnesses may feel that everyone involved is a drug dealer and why put your own life on the line when an innocent person isn't even involved?"

The new twist in intimidation is the link to gang activities, said Dr. Healey, who has surveyed prosecutors in more than 15 states. "There is the traditional witness and victim intimidation, which everybody associates with mob bookkeepers or something, but that's a very rare instance," she said. "We're talking now about the sort of intimidation that occurs in neighborhoods where a great number of people are involved in gang activity or drug sales, or personally know the participants in these activities and are in a position to be intimidated."

Gangs are a "different beast" from a single person who commits a crime, said Michael Genelin, head Deputy District Attorney of the hard-core gang division of the Los Angeles District Attorney's office.

"What you have is somebody who is being charged; perhaps he's in jail awaiting trial," Mr. Genelin said. "But then you have his friends on the outside, who, in a sense, do the bidding of the entire gang. It's the essence of conspiracy."

Brazen Criminals

In an interview, Kevin A. Ohlson, special counsel to the United States Attorney in Washington, which essentially functions as the local District Attorney in the nation's capital, said criminals had become increasingly brazen about frightening witnesses, since the lack of a witness could mean no jail time.

"The people involved in the homicide have come on the scene and posed as disinterested bystanders," even as the police are conducting interviews, Mr. Ohlson said. This is not just bravado, he added, but a clear signal that the killer knows who is talking to the police.

Some large cities, including New York, Chicago and Los Angeles, have instituted witness-protection programs, though they are more limited than the ones that confer a new identity on, say, organized-crime informers.

"We have a relocation program," said Jack Hynes, supervisor of the gang prosecution unit in Chicago's Cook County, "but it's not like what you see in *Goodfellas*, with a new name, a new birth certificate and a job in the suburbs.

Unsolved Murders

In the District of Columbia . . . police officials told a congressional subcommittee in July 1994 that one-third of all homicide cases remain unsolved because witnesses and their families are being threatened with physical harm.

"Because of this fear, a large number of cases are not going to trial," Capt. Michael Johnson told the House Judiciary Subcommittee on Crime and Criminal Justice. . . .

The congressional panel heard from a Maryland woman whose apartment had been firebombed because gangs mistakenly believed she had given information to police about a robbery. An infant died in the blaze.

Mark Curriden, *ABA Journal*, November 1994.

"It's a relocation where we might provide a first month's rent and security deposit, maybe some moving expenses. After a month or two, they're on their own. They have to carry it."

Los Angeles has a similar program, which in the 12 months that ended in June 1994 relocated 374 victims, witnesses and family members in 142 criminal cases. More than three-fourths of those cases involved gang-related crimes, according to figures compiled by the county District Attorney's office.

Typically, witnesses are moved to another neighborhood. "This is New York City," said Ms. Thompson of the Manhattan District Attorney's office. "It may be as simple as moving from one housing complex to another, from upper Manhattan to Brooklyn."

Still, the vast majority of cities, including Fort Worth, have no such programs because the costs are prohibitive.

Richard Padzieski, chief of operations and an assistant prosecutor in Detroit, said: "The closest thing I've got, if there's evidence of real danger, is to buy a bus ticket out of town. It doesn't come out of any special fund. It comes out of a fund I pay witnesses to testify."

Several cities and states, in addition to offering at least temporary protection to witnesses, have tried to increase penalties for witness intimidation. The City Council in Washington, for instance, voted in 1992 to sentence offenders to a minimum of three years in prison, with the possibility of a life term.

Several states are also allowing prosecutors to introduce pretrial statements made by witnesses who change their stories or develop amnesia on the stand. But this leaves the jury the difficult task of determining when the witness was truthful.

Los Angeles now routinely videotapes witness interviews with the police. The city's prosecutors have even conspicuously videotaped the spectators at some trials, trying to intimidate the intimidators with an open message that they are being watched. "It is amazing how gang members under those circumstances don't like to be captured on videotape," Mr. Genelin said.

In Fort Worth, the unsolved killing of Mr. Ragland has continued to haunt Ms. Moore, who now oversees gang prosecution as the deputy chief of the criminal division in the Tarrant County District Attorney's office. Tacked on the wall by her desk is a newspaper's small obituary of Mr. Ragland, who, she said, made an agonizing decision to testify in the case of a restaurant owner, Yousef Mirzadeh, who was killed during a holdup. One of the men accused in the killing was Mr. Ragland's brother-in-law.

Speaking of young Mr. Ragland, Ms. Moore said: "Junior just thought it was the right thing to do. It was a horrible crime. A most innocent, hard-working person who loved his family tremendously was killed."

And shortly after the trial in which his brother-in-law received a sentence of life in prison, Junior Ragland was dead.

"I used to be able to tell people I never lost a witness," Ms. Moore said, "but I can't say that anymore. It burned me up pretty bad. Now you have to say, 'Yes, you, too, could get killed.'"

"The growth of these organizations presents a major challenge to the quality of life in the United States and to U.S. interests."

International Crime Organizations Threaten America

Roy Godson and William J. Olson

In the following viewpoint, Roy Godson and William J. Olson argue that efficient international crime organizations (ICOs) threaten America with drug trafficking and other criminal activity. The authors maintain that these ICOs are larger and more powerful than previously known types of criminal organizations. Godson is a Georgetown University associate professor and director of the National Strategy Information Center, a research organization in Washington, D.C. Olson has served with the federal Bureau of International Narcotics Matters and is a senior fellow at the National Strategy Information Center.

As you read, consider the following questions:

1. What is the extent of the international threat from criminal organizations, in the authors' opinion?
2. How does the financial performance of Columbian drug cartels compare to businesses and nations, according to Godson and Olson?
3. According to the authors, how could foreign criminals take advantage of America's immigration stream and porous borders?

On August 18, 1989, in the middle of an adoring crowd, a gunman murdered Luis Carlos Galan, the leading candidate for the presidency of Colombia. The act shocked the nation. Political murder was not a new phenomenon in Colombia. What was new were the perpetrators. The assassin was not an individual acting alone, nor was he a member of a guerrilla group, of which Colombia has several violent examples. Instead, the assassin was a hireling, a *sicario*, acting on the orders of the Medellín Cartel, one of the world's major international criminal organizations. The murder was only the beginning. The Medellín Cartel launched a full-scale terrorist assault on the country. Public facilities and newspaper offices were bombed. Members of leading families were kidnapped. Hundreds of policemen were murdered. A national airline flight was blown up in mid-flight. The cartel waged war against the Colombian state. Its aim was to force the government to come to terms with the cartels, in effect, to share power with the drug traffickers.

The Colombian government, which had been trying to control not only Medellín groups but also the less prominent Cali group, now faced a far more violent and direct threat to its institutions. It called for help. The United States, which was already trying to support Colombian efforts, came forward with an emergency aid package and promises of more aid to follow. The United States provided upwards of $400 million in police, military, and advisory assistance over five years. These funds were intended to eliminate the major drug trafficking organizations in Colombia, and many millions more were spent to help attack the overseas operations responsible for producing and transshipping almost all the cocaine in the world.

The level of support and cooperation was unprecedented. And the threat? A drug-trafficking organization with the wealth and power to challenge the internal stability of one country while it defied the power and authority of the world's remaining superpower. Hubris? Perhaps, but the nature of the confrontation and the fact that it is not over says something fundamental about the modern world, about the nature of state power, international relations, and the stability of governments. . . .

Prolific Criminal Organizations

Whether in the developed or in the developing world, criminal organizations' scope of action and range of capabilities are undergoing a profound change. Decline in political order, deteriorating economic circumstances, a growing underground economy that habituates people to working outside the legal framework, easy access to arms, the massive flow of emigrants and refugees, and the normal difficulties involved in engendering meaningful state-to-state cooperation are working to the advantage of criminal organizations. The rise of better-organized, internationally based criminal groups with vast financial resources is creating a new threat to the stability and security of the international system. As Senator John Kerry noted, "this is new. This is something that none of us has ever experienced before. It is not ideological. It has nothing to do with right or left, but it is money-oriented, greed-based criminal enterprise that has decided to take on the lawful institutions and civilized society." The growth of these organizations presents a major challenge to the quality of life in the United States and to U.S. interests.

Foreign Criminal Operations in the United States

	Operations	Places
Chinese	Alien and heroin smuggling, extortion, gambling, prostitution	New York, the West Coast
Colombians	Cocaine trafficking	Miami, New York
Israelis	Cocaine and heroin trafficking, extortion	California, Florida, the Northeast
Jamaicans	Cocaine trafficking	Florida, New York
Japanese	Drug and gun smuggling, extortion, money laundering, prostitution	California, Hawaii
Nigerians	Heroin smuggling; credit-card, insurance, and welfare scams	New York, Houston
Russians	Arson, auto theft, burglary, counterfeiting	Dallas, Denver, Los Angeles, New York, Philadelphia, Portland

Source: Austin Case, *The World & I*, December 1993.

Although major criminal organizations pose a new and compelling challenge to national and international interests, the extent of the threat should not be exaggerated. It is clear that the wealth and power of individual organizations has grown and there are increasing signs of international links between various criminal organizations. This does not mean, however, that there is an integrated, centrally directed criminal conspiracy. The first business of criminal organizations is usually business, its promotion and protection. In this sense criminal organizations are similar to legitimate enterprises. Like the activities of their legal twins, the activities of separate "corporations" can be cooperative or competitive by turns. The long-term threat from these organizations is subtle and more insidious than images of criminal masterminds seeking to dominate the globe in some vast, shared, and centrally coordinated enterprise. . . .

Colombian Cartels and Chinese Triads

The new international organized crime groups are bigger and much more profitable than traditional [nationally based organized crime] groups. The FBI estimated in 1988 that LCN [La Cosa Nostra, the American Mafia] consisted of twenty-five independent families with a total of 2,000 members. Conversely, in 1989, Senate investigators reported estimates of as many as 100,000 members of the Colombian cocaine industry, not counting Peruvian and Bolivian groups. While it is difficult to be certain about such numbers in basically secretive organizations, the Drug Enforcement Administration computers listed the names of 24,000 persons and businesses known to be working with Colombian drug cartels in 1989. Similarly, in 1992 "conservative" estimates placed the membership of the Sun Yee On, the largest Hong Kong Triad, at 25,000, not counting its overseas members. Although not all of these were necessarily engaged in crime, the size of this one Triad indicates the potential scope of the networks available to those who are.

The scale of monetary returns on these activities also dwarfs that of traditional groups. The main driver for this is the large-scale profits generated by illegal drug trafficking. The Colombian cartels alone probably make more in a week than the American Mafia does in a year. The Colombian cartels now outperform most Fortune 500 companies. A conservative estimate of illegal drug sales at the retail, or user, level in the United States alone is $50 billion. Colombian cartels are estimated to make a profit of about $20 billion annually from these revenues. By comparison, the GDP [gross domestic product] of Colombia is only around $45 billion. The combined budgets of the governments of Colombia, Bolivia, and Peru are only about $9 billion annually. The Chinese Triads and the top manipulators of international frauds may not be making as much as the Colombians, but their profits also dwarf those of most traditional organized crime groups. . . .

The Chinese Triads—based in Hong Kong, with a few in Taiwan—are highly structured but do not direct crime from the top as do the vertically integrated cocaine cartels. Instead, Triads serve as criminal networks through which their members organize various enterprises. The Triads are largely ethnically based. They use rituals, oaths, secret ceremonies, and incentives to secure personal loyalty. Family affiliation is important at the center of major Triads. Individual membership provides credibility and influence. Members give "gifts" to their superiors in the hierarchy.

Diversity of Crimes

These groups engage in a broader range of crime than do the Colombian cartels, including drug trafficking (almost exclusively heroin), smuggling, theft, murder, extortion, credit card fraud, prostitution, and illegal gambling.

The Triads dominate the import of heroin into the United States. As with coca, worldwide production of opium has more than doubled since 1985, principally in the Golden Triangle in Southeast Asia and the Golden Crescent in Southwest Asia. Two-thirds of the world's 3,700 metric tons of opium originate in Southeast Asia, most of it in Burma. Of all the heroin available in the United States during 1991, 58 percent (up from 19 percent) came from Southeast Asia, which reflects a shift from Mexico as the primary supplier of the U.S. market. Chinese criminal groups dominate this traffic to the United States at both ends of the pipeline.

The smuggling of illegal Chinese aliens into the United States has also become a lucrative business for international organized Chinese crime. Chinese criminal organizations may earn as much as $3.1 billion a year from alien smuggling. The Immigration and Naturalization Service (INS) apprehended 6,056 illegal immigrants from China, Hong Kong, and Taiwan in 1991. An independent study indicates, however, that as many as 50,000 Chinese have been smuggled into the United States per year since 1990, an increase from less than 1,000 per year in 1983. INS officials have been quoted as estimating perhaps 100,000 enter per year.

There has been some smuggling of Chinese to the United States since the 1800s, but INS officials maintain that recent trafficking is much more sophisticated, much better organized, and unprecedented in volume. The INS has identified over ninety air routes used by smugglers through numerous foreign countries. The smugglers have begun sending whole shiploads of aliens to the United States. The U.S. Coast Guard stopped eleven seagoing vessels suspected of smuggling Chinese aliens during 1992, an unprecedented number. The number of Chinese found on board these vessels ranged from fifty-one to two hundred. The vessels were seized at locations ranging from New Bedford, Massachusetts, and Morehead City, North Carolina, on the East Coast to Long Beach, California, and Hawaii on the West.

A Culture of Secrecy

Some law enforcement officials have long been concerned that the Triads will shift more and more to the United States and

Canada when Hong Kong reverts to the People's Republic of China in 1997. Triad organizations exist in the United States. Ethnic Chinese have also formed secret societies in the United States, called *tongs*. Many tongs are legitimate business associations. However, some are fronts for criminal activities, primarily illegal gambling. Individual tong members have been linked to Triad criminal operations, such as heroin trafficking. In 1992 FBI agents raided the headquarters of the Hop Sing tong in Portland, Oregon. Among other things, they confiscated firearms easily converted to automatic fire. The weapons were believed to have been destined for the San Francisco branch of the Hong Kong–based Wo Hop To Triad.

Getting Worse

All indications are that crime by foreign gangs will worsen before law-enforcement agencies—which often do not have officers who speak the languages of immigrant criminals—can begin to solve the problem. The gangs grow so fast that they do much damage before law-enforcement agencies can even determine their existence.

Austin Case, *The World & I*, December 1993.

It is difficult, however, to get detailed information on the operations of these groups. Chinese criminal groups in the United States are strongly influenced by a "Triad culture" of secrecy and loyalty that makes them difficult to penetrate. These organizations have made significant inroads into the United States and other places where there is an overseas Chinese presence, such as in Western Europe and Asia.

Other Ethnic Groups

While the Colombian cartels and the Chinese Triads form the major ICOs, there are other groups with varying degrees of international connections that operate in the United States.

For example, Jamaican Posses, whose members come from specific neighborhoods on the island, traffic in drugs and firearms throughout the United States. Posses have been identified in most major cities on the eastern seaboard and in Cleveland, Houston, Kansas City, Los Angeles, Seattle, Anchorage, and other U.S. cities. Japanese Boryokudan (organized criminal enterprises also known as the Yakuza) launder money in the United States, smuggle guns, extort, commit fraud, and traffic in drugs. Ethnic Korean groups headquartered in Japan and affiliated with the Boryokudan control 90 percent of the flow of crystal methamphetamine ("ice") to Hawaii. Ice, a particularly debilitating drug, is appearing on the mainland West Coast.

Groups of Russians in the United States with links to the former Soviet Union are increasingly operating in the United States. They import drugs from the former Soviet Union, bring in "hit men" from abroad for contract murders, and commit jewelry theft and insurance and tax fraud. The activities of these various groups point to a rise in ethnic-based criminal organizations throughout the United States. These groups are generally limited in size, but when linked to major ICOs, as many are, they become part of and party to a much broader criminal phenomenon, which raises concerns for the future direction of criminal activity.

The Future

International criminal groups in the United States and worldwide are likely to expand. A number of factors are likely to aid their growth.

Economics of production. For small farmers in many countries, choosing to grow drug-related crops makes the most sense economically. Markets for other commodities are less profitable and less stable. In many cases, even where the necessary marketing infrastructure and expertise exist, government controls make entry into those markets difficult or impossible for peasants. At the same time, drug entrepreneurs are expanding into markets where drugs have not been a major problem in the past. Without dramatic and unlikely changes, raw materials for drug production will continue to be readily available.

Furthermore, the United States is one of the world's most lucrative markets for illegal as well as legal enterprise. It will continue to attract trade in illegal products. . . .

Immigration and Borders

Immigration streams. Ethnic criminal organizations are likely to follow immigration patterns. They do not always do so, but there has often been a strong correlation between the two. In the 1990s economic pressures and widespread ethnic turmoil are likely to generate refugees and immigrants from regions where international criminal groups are based. Between 1980 and 1990 the Asian population in the United States alone grew by 108 percent, from 3.5 million to 7.3 million. The Chinese population grew by 104 percent, from 806,000 to 1.6 million. While the vast majority of immigrants are law-abiding, criminal organizations tend to exploit immigrant communities in a variety of ways. They provide cover and concealment. Immigrant pools also provide a pool of recruits. In addition, the immigrants are usually fearful of law enforcement. Their recent experience in their country of origin makes them reluctant to cooperate with the police in their new countries. The police, moreover, historically do not provide the same degree of service to immigrants. The immigrants do not have important political connections, and the police find it difficult to cooperate with them because of their strange cultures and languages. Hence many experts anticipate increased international organized criminal activity accompanying the immigration of Russians, East Europeans, Asians, Middle Easterners, Kurds, and others.

Border Porosity. The United States' long open borders with Mexico and Canada provide ready access for criminals and illegal goods, and thousands of miles of U.S. coastline are virtually uncontrollable. The opening of free-trade areas, such as the North American Free Trade Agreement and the EC [European Community], will lower many existing safeguards and customs inspections as well.

Technology and Law Enforcement

Trends in technology. Continued advances in technology and international transportation will facilitate growth in international organized crime. The ease of modern communications makes contact among international criminal organizations easy, fast, and more secure. For example, new digital technologies make it more difficult for law enforcement bodies to intercept their communications. The movement of trillions of dollars in wire transfers each day makes it possible for many actors to evade state monitoring.

Relative disorganization of law enforcement. Preventing, disrupting, and successfully prosecuting organized crime in most parts of the world is difficult enough in the best of times. Many traditional organized criminal organizations have survived the onslaught of law enforcement organizations for decades.

Now, however, the United States and other states are faced with international criminal groups. As was described earlier, they are bigger and more powerful than most of their predecessors. They operate globally, making it impossible for law enforcement in any one jurisdiction to neutralize major parts of their activities. While some degree of cooperation exists among law enforcement agencies, and new initiatives are getting under way, many observers believe that it is inadequate to the task. In 1992, for example, a U.S. Senate report noted that there is little evidence to suggest that either U.S. or foreign law enforcement entities are currently equipped to meet the challenge of this new breed of international criminal.

Periodical Bibliography

The following articles have been selected to supplement the diverse views presented in this chapter.

Richard Bernstein	"Government Papers Offer Rare Details of the Mob's Grip on a Union," *The New York Times*, November 2, 1994.
Stephanie Brail	"Girlz in the Hood," *On the Issues*, Winter 1995.
Austin Case	"Crime Washing over America's Shores," *The World & I*, December 1993. Available from 2800 New York Ave. NE, Washington, DC 20002.
Roger H. Davis	"Cruising for Trouble: Gang-Related Drive-by Shootings," *FBI Law Enforcement Bulletin*, January 1995. Available from the FBI, Pennsylvania and Tenth Avenues NW, Washington, DC 20535.
Eric Eckholm	"Teen-Age Gangs Are Inflicting Lethal Violence on Small Cities," *The New York Times*, January 31, 1993.
Samuel Francis	"Globo-Cop," *Chronicles*, January 1995.
H. Range Hutson, Deirdre Anglin, and Michael J. Pratts Jr.	"Adolescents and Children Injured or Killed in Drive-by Shootings in Los Angeles," *The New England Journal of Medicine*, February 3, 1994.
Journal of Contemporary Criminal Justice	Special issues on organized crime, vol. 8, no. 1 (February 1992) and vol. 9, no. 3 (August 1993). Available from Dept. of Criminal Justice, California State University, 1250 Bellflower Blvd., Long Beach, CA 90840.
Barbara Kantrowitz	"Wild in the Streets," *Newsweek*, August 2, 1993.
Newsweek	"Global Mafia," December 13, 1993.
Suzanne O'Malley	"Girlz N the Hood," *Harper's Bazaar*, October 1993.
Luis J. Rodriguez	"Rekindling the Warrior," *Utne Reader*, July/August 1994.
Richard Rodriguez	"Gangstas," *Mother Jones*, January/February 1994.
Andrew E. Serwer	"The Hell's Angels' Devilish Business," *Fortune*, November 30, 1992.
William B. Sessions	"Combatting Organized Crime," *Vital Speeches of the Day*, February 15, 1993.
Claire Sterling	"Redfellas," *The New Republic*, April 11, 1994.

How Can Street Gangs Be Controlled?

Chapter Preface

In January 1995, three fourteen-year-old members of a San Diego youth gang known as the Black Mob were arrested and charged with fatally shooting a young pizza deliveryman while they were attempting to steal pizzas. Under a new California law that lowered the age minimum for adult charges from sixteen to fourteen, prosecutors sought to try one of the Black Mob youths as an adult and send him to prison for much of his adult life.

Public intolerance for such senseless violence by gang members and other youths has grown. According to an October 1993 *USA Today*/CNN/Gallup survey, 73 percent of respondents said juveniles who commit violent crimes should be punished as adults. The following month, Illinois senator Carol Moseley-Braun successfully led a campaign to amend the federal Omnibus Anti-Crime Bill to allow offenders as young as thirteen to be tried as adults for certain violent crimes.

Moseley-Braun and others contend that the juvenile justice system has been too soft on violent youths, dispensing probation more often than incarceration. Thus, they argue, kids may get the impression that they will not be punished and may therefore be tempted to commit serious crimes. As *San Diego Union-Tribune* columnist Joseph Perkins writes, "Maybe while violent young offenders are behind bars, they will commit themselves to treading on the straight and narrow."

But many critics condemn strict sanctions as ineffective or discriminatory. Author and former gang member Luis J. Rodriguez argues, "No 'three strikes, you're out,' no trying children as adults, no increased prison spending will address [the gang problem]." According to Rodriguez and others, these measures fail to reduce the constant pressures on at-risk youths to join gangs. Others point out that in California, many youths spend more time incarcerated than do adults convicted of similar crimes, and that the same holds true in Utah for many minority youths compared to nonminority youths.

Because of their age, predatory young teens and their brutal acts confound many communities. The effort to punish violent gang youths harshly is among the issues debated in this chapter on measures to control street gangs and related crime and violence.

> *"What is the message that I want to relay to the armed gangs? . . . You do not have the support of the community, and you will never win."*

Eradicate the Gang Culture

Ben Garza

Ben Garza is a San Jose, California, father whose teenage son was paralyzed from the waist down in a drive-by shooting. In the following viewpoint, Garza asserts that society must confront the problem of gangs and end gangs' attractiveness to youths. He warns children to have nothing to do with gangs and to direct their interests toward school, work, and other productive activities. Garza calls for an end to the glorification of violence in American culture and music, and he maintains that there should be no pity toward gang members who hurt others and who choose not to reform.

As you read, consider the following questions:

1. In Garza's opinion, what should be the proper use of the Constitution regarding gangs and violence?
2. How can the Chicano movement work against gangsterism, in the author's opinion?
3. According to Garza, what skills should youths acquire?

Ben Garza, "Gangs: Good for Nothing," *San Jose Mercury News*, December 29, 1993. Reprinted with permission.

I came home from work on Dec. 17, 1993, to learn, from the messages on my phone, that my son had been shot in a gang-related drive-by shooting only two hours before. The message was to come immediately to the hospital.

My son was 16 years old, my only son. I have no daughters. He was hit four times: twice in his leg, once in his neck and once in his lungs. He was at a phone booth when a car drove by and the occupants opened fire. This was not the Christmas present I expected.

Driving to the hospital, I kept thinking about the worst possible things. I told myself that I had to keep calm and that I had to stay mentally intact because my son was going to need all the support he could get from me, his family and from his friends.

When I got to the emergency room, I saw from a distance the body of my son laid out on a stretcher. I could not see his face from this point, but the sheets had blood on them.

The doctor first talked to me so that I would not be shocked and said that my son was paralyzed. From where I stood he looked dead, which sent chills through my body.

I went to talk to the doctor who was attending him. He was a young man about my age. I told him that my son was my only family and to do his best. His remarks were not encouraging. I left the hospital, and it was cold outside. I kept asking why it had happened to my son. Why me, and what have we done to deserve this?

Feeling Guilty

I kept blaming myself for working so many long hours and having little time to be with my son. My son had become involved with a gang; I did not learn about it until too late. I kept blaming myself, thinking that I was responsible for his being in the wrong place at the wrong time.

My instinct was to find out who those gang members were and to give them the same treatment that they had given my son. Anger dominated my thinking.

The next morning, I immediately called the hospital and asked how my son was doing. To my surprise he was on the other end of the line and started talking to me. That lifted my hopes very high. My son survived four bullets. It was a miracle.

What is the message that I want to clearly relay to every parent in regard to this violent trend that we are seeing among our youth?

Perhaps the most important question that every one of you should ask your children should be whether they are involved in gangs, whether they have easy access to guns, and whether they would use them in resolving a conflict among themselves or against another person.

Also, our Constitution must have the power to prohibit the development of violent culture and the development of a violent ideology, including violent music, in our society.

If it doesn't have that power, then our Constitution is much too old and out of date to deal with the new age and time; in essence, it is worthless. No lawyer, politician or legal rights groups should use the Constitution for the sole purpose of defending the forces responsible for the violence that is spreading in our society.

A Culture of Death and Terror

My 30-year-old son, Jesus, is dead at the hands of the Fourth Street gang from the Pico Gardens housing project in [East Los Angeles].

It was a despicable and senseless murder. He was gunned down inside his car as the killers robbed him. I learned that he defended himself but he never had a chance. He was shot in the back of the head, the stomach and legs. I was able to see him still breathing, battling for his life, but he succumbed.

I am outraged. Like the thousands of innocent people killed during the last twelve years by gang violence, he had not lived his full life. He leaves four children, from two months to ten years old, to become dependent on a single parent. . . .

The [gang] situation has our community and the larger society in a quandary. What do we do—love them unconditionally and turn the other cheek? My son's killers were not children. They are, I have learned, in their mid-twenties; one was just released because of insufficient evidence in another murder. . . .

Make no mistake, our community has been invaded by a culture of death and terror; it is thriving. Without "foreign aid" in the billions for our community war zones, there will be no peace.

Javier Rodriguez H., *Los Angeles Times*, April 8, 1993.

What is the message that I want to relay to the armed gangs? The message must be clear. You do not have the support of the community, and you will never win. If you have been increasing in size and in activity, it is because the existing state has cut so much in the necessary social services and programs where our children once benefited, leaving them vulnerable.

You take advantage of the ignorance of our youth. For you, our children have only one purpose—to be used as tools and as thugs to promote your illegal activities.

Gangsterism must be replaced by a new Chicano-Mexicano

Movement—a new militant and disciplined organization of Brown Beret youth who will work against drugs, gang warfare and criminal activity and for education. There is nothing wrong in having Chicano pride when we know that it will create productive youth in our part of the society.

What is the message I want to relay to the youth? Don't be stupid and foolish. Do not let anyone lead you by the nose with your eyes and mind closed. Violence never did resolve anything among our people; it only brought about more violence.

For those of you who want to join a gang or are in one, you must ask yourself, "How long do I want to live?"

What all of you need is not the skill of knowing how to pull the trigger against one another but the skill in working a computer; learning to read, write and express yourself; learning to be productive inside industry; learning to be political and fighting for your human rights.

As youth you deserve to have a fair share of the resources that society produces. You must learn to love your community and respect your parents and elders and learn to be cooperative and not compete against each other in the most violent and deadly ways.

Go to the corporations and say, "Here we are; we are ready to work." Force the corporations to provide youth with job training. Go to the colleges and say, "Here we are; we are ready to study." Force the schools to teach you even if it means fighting politically until they see that you do have the right to an education—even if you are poor. Go into the community and say, "Here we are; we are ready to serve in a good cause." Force the community to organize youth conferences, youth fairs and youth tours of the universities and force the politicians to address the youth.

Nobody ever will call the youth "gangsters" when everyone knows that they are demanding the right things in life.

Losing Fear

And to all of the people who are fed up with gangs and violence, my message is this: You should not be afraid to speak or to expose these negative gangs in our society and neighborhoods. We must lose the fear that terrorism has us under and fight back by exposing violent gang members. Let us be fair and give the gang member an alternative, a chance to reform, to put down the guns and to learn a new way of life.

But we should have no pity for those who do not want to reform and who are killing and hurting our children, our families, brothers and sisters, no matter what color they come in. There is nothing cool about these thugs.

We need to boycott the rappers who glorify violence and dirty language. We need to lose our fear and turn in those who are using guns against the people in general and especially against our people in the barrio and ghetto.

If we go down, let us go down fighting with everything in our power, especially with the truth—that thugs are not worth a cent to our people and country and much less to our youth.

The shooting of my son has won a new recruit against these armed thugs. Our youth can have no peace as long as the gangs exist.

The truth is that we in the barrio and ghetto do not want drugs or the gangs any more than the general society does. It is time to unite against thugs.

"If we think they're human beings, then our strategy is . . . clear—love, employment, opportunity, school, recreation, care."

Treat Gang Members as Human Beings to Reform Them

Greg Boyle, interviewed by Sharon R. Bard

Greg Boyle is a Jesuit priest at Dolores Mission Church in East Los Angeles who is well known for his efforts to help gang members and other youths. In the following viewpoint, an interview by Sharon R. Bard, Boyle argues that gang youths are human beings who must be treated with love and compassion. Boyle contends that poverty and despair are prime reasons why youths join gangs and that they sorely need jobs and other opportunities. Bard is an educational consultant and freelance writer in Sonoma County, California.

As you read, consider the following questions:

1. How do gang youths react when confronted by adults who want to help them, in Boyle's experience?
2. According to the author, how have people in his community organized against gangs?
3. Why was the *60 Minutes* segment on gangs so effective, according to Boyle?

Greg Boyle, interviewed by Sharon R. Bard, "Gang Life," *Creation Spirituality*, Spring 1994. Reprinted with permission.

Bard: Why did you decide to minister to gangs?

Boyle: I wanted to work with the poor and there was no group more poor than those people of Dolores Mission in East Los Angeles. I got involved in the world of gangs quite by accident, creating an alternative school and then a jobs program. I now speak English, Spanish, and a whole other thing which is more than just words and language.

Initially, these kids weren't very welcoming. Many gangs sold drugs and were hyper-paranoid about snitches. I made a point of learning everybody's names and as I walked past someone I could hear him say, "Hey, the priest knows our names." When kids got shot I'd go to the hospital, and if a kid was locked up I'd visit him in jail.

We're dealing with an enormously complex social ill that must be addressed on many fronts such as poverty, dysfunctional family, despair, boredom, unemployment, and failure of schools. Although law enforcement plays an important role, the police cannot address root causes. My strategy with gangs is to ask "Is this activity good, true, morally correct, and loving?" Whether it's successful or not is somebody else's issue, or God's task.

They Are Human Beings

These kids are human beings. They're interesting, warm, loving, tender, intelligent, and wildly imaginative. The prevailing culture's sense of them is quite distorted.

A gang member on my work crew was shot in the head and became brain-dead. After being in intensive care for several days, his family agreed to donate his heart, kidney, and liver. As two nurses wheeled him to the operating room, one turned to the other and said, "Who would want this monster's heart?" The other nurse replied, "How dare you say that, you don't even know this kid. Didn't you see his girlfriend sitting by his bed for three days? Didn't you see all the friends come and kiss him and caress him and cry and say goodbye?" She understood what we're dealing with here.

This kid was the oldest of five. I buried his father of a heroin overdose about five years ago. His mother was a coolie head, which means she smoked cools, PCP. All his younger brothers and sisters were taken away and put in foster homes. He was a kid who was dealt an extraordinarily bad hand. Given all that, I thought he played it quite well.

Is this ability to empathize with someone who's so different and perhaps hostile a teachable one? Most people want to stay away from gangs rather than reach out to them.

We pay a tremendous price for ignorance. Only knowledge breaks through it. During the *60 Minutes* segment [featuring Boyle in April 1992], Mike Wallace admitted, "I came here expecting to find monsters, and that's not at all what I found."

We must be open to the truth, and the truth is just seeing these kids. Because if we think these kids are monsters, then our strategy as a society will be abundantly clear—wipe them out, lock them up, exterminate them. But if we think they're human beings, then our strategy is equally clear—love, employment, opportunity, school, recreation, care. The solution is actually lived out at the grass roots level by confronting these kids with the experience most foreign to them . . . a loving, caring adult.

Tougher to Care

What about being tough on crime? Let me be clear: I hate crime. I hate drugs. I hate children murdering children. But I know from experience that it doesn't take guts to put money into inhumane, punishment-driven institutions. In fact, such policies make our communities even less safe. It's tougher to walk these streets, to listen to young people, to respect them and help fight for their well-being. It's tougher to care.

Luis J. Rodriguez, *The Nation*, November 21, 1994.

Don't they resist?

Not usually. They're human beings and it's what they're most starving for. If there is resistance at first, it would probably come from a bad experience with adults.

One day Speedy, a member of the Mob Crew, told me, "You know, G, I just don't care whether I live or die." "Look, mijo," I said, "a lot of us feel this at one time or another in our lives. The only thing I can tell you right now is I care whether you live or die."

A Woman's Aid

He left and returned two hours later, telling me he walked Anna home. I know Anna lived in enemy territory and walking her home was suicidal. Speedy was chased by enemies who threw bottles at him, and as he escaped he ran into Yolanda, a woman in our mother's group committed to peace in the barrio. Speedy and Yolanda only knew each other by sight. Yet she knew enough to know he's a gang member who shouldn't be in that neck of the woods. She stopped him and said in Spanish, "What are you doing here? I really worry about you being here at this time of night." And then she added, "If anything ever happened to you it would just break my heart in half." "You know what, G?" Speedy told me, "that shit made me feel good."

Well, what a small thing! This woman was able to communicate care and love to a kid she doesn't even know. And that was, I sensed, for that night, the slenderest thread that kept that kid connected to his own future, and to a love for life and all the things human beings need to live from one day to the next.

Deep Despair

Do you feel much despair?

I've never actually felt despair, although I've felt frustrated and angry. I've buried twenty-six kids. At all the funerals, I corner a kid who's out in the parking lot by himself crying and smoking a cigarette. Thinking maybe he'll be vulnerable to hear something for the first time, I put my arm around him and say, "You know, mijo, I never want to see you lying in a casket at sixteen." What's eerie to me is these guys always say the same one or two things: "Why not," or "You gotta die sometime." Both are indicators of a very deep and pressing despair.

I got a letter from a kid who's locked up. I've never met him although I've written him for a number of years. His letter made me cry:

> Dear G: Hello, it's me, José, dropping a few lines down your way just to see what's up. I'm back at Norwalk, for stabbing a ward at Nelles [youth correctional facilities in the Los Angeles area]. I had to. I thank you for everything. Really I do. I'm still a Christian, I'm not going to quit. If I could gang-bang and die, then I could do it for our Lord.

> I wish I could see and talk to you. I'll be out to work with you soon. It's no big thing. My baby sister was killed by Eighteenth Street. I'm out for blood right now. I'm on lockdown right now. I got choir right now. I must close now. But not forever. Not for long. Bye and take care of yourself. I'm praying for you, too.

It amazes me that this kid who stabbed somebody simply says, "I had to." And then two thirds of the way into the letter he mentions in just one line that his baby sister was killed by Eighteenth Street. How enormously complex and painful this all is! He was making so many improvements. The kid he stabbed probably was from Eighteenth Street. Packed in this kind of letter, printed like a fifth grader with the "n's" backwards, are volumes about the depth of his pain and conflict.

The *Caminatas*

Have the parishioners supported your projects?

When I first got to Dolores Mission there were a number of disgruntled parishioners who were uncomfortable because gang members would hang around the grounds. We had a parish meeting and the majority said, "We need to own this situation because it's what God would want us to do." It was an extraordinary moment and from then on, we never had a single problem.

Recently, groups of women have started *caminatas*. They walk all night long on the weekends, in packs, in the projects. Their mission is dangerous and very disarming. Yet their presence makes the guys put their guns away and go inside. Part of the *caminatas'* message is, "You are not the enemy. You are our sons, but we won't allow you to kill each other." They're a force to be reckoned with.

The caminatas *are a new slant on vigilantes—defense through love.*

It is loving. These same women organized a five hundred strong candlelight procession where the theme was: disarm your sons—go into their room, lift up the mattress, get the Uzi and bring it to the church. This is very different from the standard procedure in most communities where gang members are seen as our enemy and we are encouraged to oppose them. These women see the kids are not evil but are in trouble. Because their analysis of the problem is good, their response is good. And the guys clearly see it as an ultimate act of love.

Addressing Poverty

Then who are the real enemies?

I think the enemy is poverty. After the 1992 uprising in L.A. I helped moderate a dialogue between city kids and powerful community organizers. These leaders said, "We need a good prevention program." For them, moral compasses were out of whack. "We need to get the kids back in shape, on course, catch them early and keep repeating to them, 'Just say no to gangs'." All of this was, of course, said in front of the gangs.

A seventeen-year-old African American male stood up. In a very gentle and wise tone he said to Senator John D. Rockefeller, "I really appreciate the fact that you want to have a gang prevention program for my younger brother. But what good will it do him if my mother and father don't have a job, and can't feed us, pay the rent, or take care of us?"

To me, that was just so astute. If we can relieve tension on the economic level, then kids will start to have a sense of the future. It's not a question of the bad kids saying "yes" to gangs and the good kids saying "no." If you're stressed out, if your despair is deep enough, you will become a gang member.

After this forum, I met with Disney merchandising and suggested they take over an empty factory and hire guys from the area to do the manufacturing. "That's a dead-end job," the executive told me. But a dead-end job to him is the ticket out of the projects for a gang member. It gives him a reason to get up in the morning and a reason not to gangbang at night.

Even if they would make more money dealing drugs than making minimum wage?

That's a myth. Surprisingly, they'll drop the sale of drugs and accept a job at Pizza Hut. One night after a call from a prestigious firm, I rode my bike to Pico Garden's Fifth Street where two guys had just made a very lucrative crack sale and were counting their bills.

"You've got this job offer," I told them. "You start tomorrow morning. It pays six dollars an hour and you need to wear a tie. You'll have two bosses. One you'll meet tomorrow, and one you're staring at right now. The rules: No hanging (kicking it with the homeys; i.e., fellow gang members), banging (gang activity: writing on walls to drive-by shootings) or slanging (selling crack)." These guys make hundreds of dollars a day, yet the only thing they said to me was, "Hook us up."

Sometimes a kid just doesn't have enough of what it takes inside to be able to stick with a job. He might go back to selling drugs. You have to do a lot of hand-holding and pummeling him with affirmation and strokes until he discovers he has enough to continue.

Since your interview on 60 Minutes *and the riots which occurred after the first Rodney King trial, have you observed a positive response toward economic assistance in the community?*

Yes. What was so effective about *60 Minutes* was that it promoted a human face on this issue. Without fail from the amount of mail I still get, people are saying, "I had no idea that these were human beings. People who cry, have feelings and have been dealt a bad hand by and large." So in the end this can only issue in good strategies. Because it's the truth. And in the end I think we all will benefit, if we listen to our hearts.

*"Gang offenses can be dealt with, contained,
policed, and prosecuted."*

Tough Laws Should
Target Gangs

Michael Genelin

Michael Genelin is the head deputy of the Hardcore Gang
Division in the Los Angeles District Attorney's Office. In the
following viewpoint, Genelin maintains that there are many
ways for law enforcement and prosecutors to suppress gang
crime. Genelin argues that appropriate strategies include interagency task forces, strict laws to target gangs, and the effective
use of police and prosecutors.

As you read, consider the following questions:

1. What is vertical prosecution, as described by Genelin?
2. According to Genelin, why does the Los Angeles gang task
   force advocate a community policing approach?
3. According to the author, how did authorities in Los Angeles
   overcome a limitation of the STEP Act?

From *The Gang Intervention Handbook* (pp. 417-19, 421-26), edited by A.P. Goldstein and
C.R. Huff, 1993, Champaign, IL: Research Press. Copyright 1993 by the authors. Adapted
by permission.

The word *gang* brings shudders to the community and community law enforcement officials alike. Mention gangs and the media go wild, disseminating images of vicious young thugs roaming neighborhoods and preying on unsuspecting citizens. Certainly, gangs are dangerous. And granted, gangs are cause for public concern—particularly, law enforcement concern. But gang offenses can be dealt with, contained, policed, and prosecuted. The questions are, How do we deal with the gang issue in terms of both public awareness and police and prosecution concerns? How do we successfully identify, prosecute, and incarcerate the criminal gang member? and, How can we "partner" with the public to help us in this endeavor?

Gangs are a unique problem in prosecution. We know that multiple criminals acting with a singularity of purpose create greater problems than criminals acting alone. Conspiracies, or multiple felons acting together, have a larger, longer reach. We certainly know that group action can terrorize. At the street gang level, the use of gang colors, gang clothing, gang signs, graffiti plastered all over buildings, and the gang's willingness to use force can intimidate neighborhoods. The fact is that, according to Kenneth Ehrensoft, the "key responsibility for bringing . . . gang offenders to justice, protecting the community, and thereby serving its best interest, has been placed on the county prosecutor or district attorney in conjunction with the police officer." The question then becomes, How do we exercise that responsibility?

Hard-Core Gang Members

One underlying problem concerns reluctance on the part of government authorities to confess that a gang crime issue exists. Acknowledging a problem might bring citizen protest or criticism and a possible challenge at the polls. However, research has revealed that gang members are more likely to commit a multitude of crimes—and commit them more often—than are non–gang members. And the more dedicated members are to the gang, the more hard-core, the more likely those gang members are to commit many more crimes. Essentially, hard-core gang members are charged with 70% more offenses than other gang members. Before such individuals can be successfully identified and prosecuted, all of the agencies concerned must agree that an issue confronts them. Only then may the extent of the gang threat in any given jurisdiction be determined and a systematic approach to gang intervention be undertaken. . . .

The Los Angeles Approach

An example of a policy toward gang prosecutions can be taken from the Los Angeles County District Attorney's Office. The stated objective was to use every opportunity to remove gang members from the streets. This objective was achieved by identifying street gang members at the time of filing [a charge]. Their gang membership was then used as an aggravating factor at the time of sentencing to minimize case settlements and aggressively seek maximum sentences.

Reprinted by permission of Chuck Asay and Creators Syndicate.

On the basis of perceived public need, certain assumptions were made in promulgating the policy. It was assumed that gang members are more dangerous than typical individual criminals. It logically followed, then, that they should be incarcerated for as long as possible. This policy was to be followed with identified gang members *irrespective of whether the current offense was gang related*—even at the misdemeanor level. Four program stages were established: (a) the identification of a defendant as a member of a criminal street gang, (b) special guidelines for filing and case settlement, (c) advocacy for maximum custody at sentencing, and (d) a probation violation program for gang offenders. Every effort was made to keep the defendant in custody during the pendency of the case through the use of high bail. Further, if the defendant was convicted and placed on probation, special conditions of probation were instituted (i.e., the defendant could not associate with other members of the gang, was prohibited from wearing colors, was subject to search conditions).

The Los Angeles policy was based on an assessment of what gang members are and how the agency wanted to deal with them, as well as on an acknowledgment that there are not enough gang prosecutors in Los Angeles to prosecute all the gang members committing crimes. Through this strict approach to case settlement and sentencing postures, a tone for gang prosecutions for the entire office was set. The policy also served as a declaration for the courts and the public about what was needed in the gang prosecution and sentencing processes.

Experienced Prosecutors

A policy declaration, no matter how well followed, is generally not enough. Expertise, and its utilization, is the next step. Why? Because gang cases are unique. They require special prosecutors who have been trained in gang prosecution techniques and who can vertically prosecute gang members.

Vertical prosecution units have existed for some time. The career criminal units set up in the 1960s to prosecute violent recidivists had a similar rationale: The prosecutor who files a case, interviews the witnesses, and commences conserving and enhancing the evidence throughout the prosecution knows that case from the ground up. The expertise of this prosecutor, then, will maximize case results. For example, we know that gang members intimidate witnesses. A prosecutor's early rapport with these witnesses is essential to counter the fear factor. In addition, gang members speak street jargon (e.g., Caló) that a trained prosecutor can understand and use. Witness protection in gang cases is another consideration that requires the trained gang prosecutor's experience. . . .

Interagency Cooperation

If [city] agencies can openly articulate a gang problem, they should be willing to interact on an ongoing basis to share problems, information, and potential solutions. An example, again, can be taken from a group currently in existence in Los Angeles—the Los Angeles Interagency Gang Task Force.

In 1980 gang violence in Los Angeles rose to new heights. The agencies concerned with gang suppression formed gang-specific units to target the problem: the District Attorney's Office formed its Hardcore Prosecution Division, the Sheriff's Department formed Operation Safe Streets, the Los Angeles Police Department formed its Community Resources Against Street Hoodlums (CRASH) Division, and the Probation Department formed high-intensity suppression units to supervise gang members. Division representatives from these groups decided to meet on an ongoing basis as the Los Angeles Interagency Gang Task Force. A permanent liaison was established with the schools, the Mayor's Office, the Department of Paroles, the Board of Supervisors, the Los Angeles City Attorney's Office, and other agencies. . . .

Gang Reporting, Evaluation, and Tracking

A concrete result of agencies' involvement in the task force has been the development of the Gang Reporting, Evaluation, and Tracking (GREAT) information system. All identified gang members in Los Angeles are logged into the program's computer, along with their known associates (homeboys), aliases, and family—virtually all the information on the individual pertinent to his or her gang membership and criminality. As a result of the GREAT program, police can immediately tap into a gang member's background. Prosecutors know exactly what type of defendant or defense witness is being called and can more clearly articulate how gang membership relates to the crime in question.

But what has this continuing consortium of gang-interested groups meant to the community? The task force recognized the alienation between police and the communities that they serve, so it strongly urged that law enforcement agencies in the county adopt community-based policy strategies within their jurisdictions. It also recognized the need for community mobilization and suggested that law enforcement agencies initiate and facilitate community gang prevention efforts as a means of reducing that alienation. This policy has led to the development of focused, reasoned responses targeted toward specific problem-solving efforts. A closer look is in order.

The Reduction of Street Violence Program

The Reduction of Street Violence Program (RSVP) approach was created as a result of planning suggested by the task force. In this particular case, a high-risk gang area was the focus. The police in this area interacted on a daily basis with local, nongovernmental gang-interested groups to determine where danger zones existed in the community. As a result of the information obtained, the police shifted more personnel to these areas. Extra patrols were also established in parks to provide community residents with safe havens. In addition, school antigang programs were developed and instituted in conjunction with antidrug programs such as DARE (Drug Abuse Resistance Education) and SANE (Substance Abuse Narcotics Education). Gang violence counselors and the police attempted to cool off gang animosities. The results of these cooperative efforts were that gang crime was suppressed to a significant degree.

Another example of how cooperation between agencies and communities can help in gang suppression and intervention is the case of East Los Angeles. In 1990 the number of gang-related crimes rose dramatically in the East Los Angeles area after having been under control for a long time. A local political action group requested law enforcement assistance. The Probation Department, the Los Angeles County Sheriff's Department, and the Los Angeles County District Attorney's Office brought their particular expertise to bear on the situation.

No Tolerance

Currently, Utah has in place a statute providing stiff mandatory sentences for crimes involving two or more individuals. Selected offenses, such as assault, homicide and drug-related crimes, committed by three or more individuals also are subject to mandatory enhanced penalties. The Salt Lake County attorney believes these statutes deliver a strong message that gang violence will not be tolerated.

Salvador A. Mendez, *Corrections Today*, July 1992.

Initial discussions between the agencies and the community members revealed the following: Essentially, the local hard-core gang "veteranos" had been put in prison years before—and the gangs had gone dormant. However, now the veteranos were out and active again, urging renewed gang warfare. The result was that over 30 gang murders were committed in that area within less than a year. This crisis was exacerbated by large-scale immigration from Mexico and Central America. Some of these new arrivals were contesting the established groups for turf, again resulting in increased violence in the area.

The initial approach involved focusing on the prison returnees. A number of them were rearrested for new crimes. Gang members on probation were monitored more intensely—in fact, it was made clear to them that they were being closely watched because of their gang involvement. Additional gang community workers were brought into the area to monitor disputes. The Los Angeles County Sheriff's Department also brought in additional gang-focused deputies, particularly Gang Enforcement Teams (GETs), which were highly mobile and active in their gang contacts. The Los Angeles County District Attorney's Office contributed an added prosecutor to focus solely on the East Los Angeles arrests and prosecutions and to provide support to the police. Community action by local civilian antigang groups, such as antigraffiti efforts and antigang rallies, was supported. Finally, Street Terrorism Enforcement and Prevention Act (STEP) procedures were initiated.

The Los Angeles County District Attorney's Office was one of the primary forces behind the passage, in 1989, of the Street Terrorism Enforcement and Prevention Act. Essentially, the statute declared that if (a) an individual actively participated in a criminal street gang, (b) had knowledge that the gang's members had engaged in a pattern of criminal activity (i.e., committed multiple crimes of murder, robbery, felonious assaults, etc.) over a 3-year period, and (c) that individual promoted felonious criminal conduct or assisted members of the gang in such conduct, then he or she was also guilty of a separate felony. There was a limitation on these sections: Prosecutors had to prove that gang members had knowledge that they were participating in a criminal street gang. However, that hurdle was overcome by the district attorney. The district attorney developed a notice that was printed by the District Attorney's Office and served to targeted gang members by police officers. This notice was written in both English and Spanish and informed the gang members that they were in a criminal street gang, why the gang had been designated a criminal street gang, and what the consequences of remaining in a criminal street gang were. After word got out, when gang members saw police officers approaching them they would run, knowing that otherwise they were going to be served. But the result of the measure is clear—gang crime in the targeted area has started to level off.

Taking Back a Park

We have already discussed the STEP Act. Clearly, it was devised to fit a prosecutorial need—gang suppression. Prosecutors' determination to write and enact the law stemmed from the perception that adequate tools were unavailable and had to be created. The perception was acted on by writing the statute, going to the legislature, explaining the need, and arguing for its enactment.

There are other similar examples of prosecutors' aggressive response to gang violence through the development of a law or ordinance. In one community, for example, two rival criminal street gangs were fighting for control of a park. As a result, community residents were afraid to use the park, virtually abandoning it to the gang members. Municipalities have a special interest in controlling their parks, parks being where their children play. It was apparent that this particular community was in an emergency situation. Residents had actually been shot in the crossfire of the two gangs. But the city was a small one with a tax base that made 24-hour patrolling an onerous financial burden. The solution was an ordinance, written to prevent criminal street gang members from entering the park. The ordinance was simple in form but complex in ramification.

The ordinance, like the STEP Act, indicated that it only applied to criminal street gangs, as defined within the statute. A gang member's entering the park was established as an infraction of the ordinance, meaning that the ordinance would be enforced through the serving of citations, much like a traffic ticket. Why just a citation? Because the objective was not to put more people in jail, but to tell gang members that law enforcement had put them under a microscope. The citation served as a warning that they were being watched. That first rung on the enforcement ladder to jail also involved a large chunk out of their pocketbooks. Early indications are that gang members now give the park a wide berth. . . .

Many Options

It is clear that a large range of options are available for the prosecutor dealing with gang crimes. Options can include providing support for victims of gang crimes and protection for witnesses; utilizing data-tracking systems, vertical prosecution techniques, and vertical prosecution divisions; interceding with the schools and communities; and passing special laws to deal with specific gang problems.

Assisting in the development of long-term, comprehensive, and coordinated strategies that include prevention and early intervention for youth at risk is not outside prosecutors' ambit. Developing fundamental reforms to the system, most particularly the juvenile justice system, is a necessary task. And supporting community mobilization or interacting with the public outside the court system may be prosecutors' new mission. In responding to law enforcement and community needs, prosecutors combining flexibility with a creative imagination can generate solutions to even such troubling criminal issues as those generated by criminal street gangs.

"The problem of teenage crime cannot be solved exclusively by law enforcement attempts to destroy youth gangs."

Tough Laws Should Not Target Gangs

Jeffrey J. Mayer

A hard-line strategy against gangs is an incorrect, counterproductive approach, Jeffrey J. Mayer argues in the following viewpoint. Mayer contends that broad definitions used to identify gang members could include youths who are not gang members or who are not involved at all in gang crimes. Mayer asserts that many such youths could be unjustly punished by tough sanctions, such as imprisonment. Mayer thus advocates laws that target individual criminals but disregard possible gang connections. Mayer is a litigator for the law firm of Raymond and Prokop in Birmingham, Michigan.

As you read, consider the following questions:

1. Why are gang symbols and youths' association with gangs often unrelated to criminal purpose, according to Mayer?
2. According to the author, what is wrong with the police practice of "flipping" suspected gang members?
3. In Mayer's opinion, why should criminals be treated as individuals rather than as gang members?

From Jeffrey J. Mayer, "Individual Moral Responsibility and the Criminalization of Youth Gangs," *Wake Forest Law Review*, vol. 28, no. 4 (Winter 1993), pages 943-86. Reprinted with permission.

The last two decades have witnessed unprecedented youth violence. Much of the youth violence has been savage. A prominent cause of the violence, according to many observers, is the supposedly dramatic expansion in the number and power of youth street gangs. Public fascination with these gangs is intense. Newspapers, television, and films have explored extensively the African-American gangs of Los Angeles, particularly the notorious Crips and Bloods. Other ethnic groups and their youth gangs are beginning to receive the same type of obsessive scrutiny. Social scientists and journalists have in turn conducted extensive field research (urban ethnology) into gangs.

Public Panic

The popular interest in gangs generally focuses on their elimination. Gangs are routinely portrayed as an alien presence in otherwise stable communities. For most people, gangs represent a breakdown of the moral order, an evil in which racial or ethnic ties have been perverted for criminal gain. Gangs frighten the public because they appear to use one of the most comforting aspects of life, deep-rooted personal ties, to foster campaigns of invasive and disruptive violence. Reflecting the public concern over the perceived moral breakdown, a parent in Atlanta explained:

> The official position is that the mayors and police departments have gangs under control, when in fact they don't have control of the streets. . . . They [gangs] are not loosely knit. They are highly disciplined and they are protective of their turf. They are beginning to stretch out into suburban areas.

As a result of the public panic, a military style response has been forthcoming. Legislative and prosecutorial efforts designed to identify and attack youth gangs are a high priority at the federal, state, and local level. Police and prosecutors have devised strategies to identify and destroy the allegedly ruthless and immoral street gangs. Numerous new laws also establish procedures for the identification and destruction of gangs and gang members. What distinguishes the anti-gang initiatives from standard anti-crime efforts is the emphasis on external indicia of social association. Since gangs are presumptively tightly knit criminal conspiracies, gang symbols indicate social deviance and criminal responsibility.

According to the United States Justice Department, for example, the goal is to "[t]ake back the streets and liberate our neighborhoods from the tyranny of fear." This and other anti-gang initiatives are defined expressly [here by former U.S. Attorney General Dick Thornburgh] as a war against an alien presence:

> [O]ur hearts lifted as joint military operations won a great victory over violence and aggression in the Persian Gulf. That

victory [is] a textbook example of military might brought to bear upon a ruthless enemy. . . .

[N]ow we launch a coordinated attack on drug dealers, gangs, and criminal predators to free the target area of crime by combined Federal, State and local law enforcement.

Similarly, state legislation presenting anti-gang initiatives such as California's "Street Terrorism Enforcement and Prevention Act" utilizes military language to highlight a warlike effort.

Misguided Efforts

These warlike efforts are misguided and likely to aggravate the epidemic of youth violence. The reality is that the extent of the gang problem, as even hard-line anti-gang crusaders admit, "is unknown except in large cities like Los Angeles, New York and Chicago," according to Edward F. Connors. Even in these major cities, a clear understanding of the gang problem is elusive due to the indistinguishability of social ties and criminal purposes in many teenage social groups, as well as the racial and political factors which are inherently involved in anti-gang initiatives. While a declaration of war against gangs may be psychologically gratifying, the salient question is whether such a declaration can effectively make our streets safer—let alone benefit the youths subsequently arrested and incarcerated. Inadequate consideration has been given to the issue.

The United States is home to many organized criminal conspiracies, some organized around ethnic ties and others around a common "gang" identity. This viewpoint . . . emphatically rejects the assertion that law enforcement should not address the epidemic of youth crime by prosecuting and incarcerating violent felons. While teenage criminality is not simply a matter of bad behavior, individuals, including the youths at the center of the supposed street gang crisis, should bear individual moral responsibility for the acts they commit.

Criminal liability should be ascribed according to traditional legal principles and not to gangs as social entities, as proposed in various anti-gang initiatives. Individuals who commit violent acts should be held responsible for those acts, regardless of extenuating circumstances such as unemployment, domestic strife, or educational neglect. Ascribing criminal responsibility in this manner is proper for both practical and moral reasons.

Imprisonment

An urgent and well-founded desire to control street crime cannot relieve law enforcement from the practical impact of a widespread crackdown. The problem of teenage crime cannot be solved exclusively by law enforcement attempts to destroy youth gangs. Gangs are, and always have been, groups of youths formed for many of the same motives that youths have always organized themselves—friendship and social identity as well as the pursuit of delinquent or criminal activities. Furthermore, American prisons are vastly overcrowded, and the public resists requests to fund construction of more prisons. Even when the public is willing to fund additional construction, people are unwilling to permit construction in their neighborhoods. Consequently, an indiscriminate crackdown on gangs will result in more and younger briefly incarcerated teenagers and children, some of whom may be guilty only of associating with violent criminals. Since imprisonment alone does not rehabilitate, the almost certain result of incarceration for even a brief period is the creation of a hard-core criminal.

Gang Lists

In Los Angeles County, nearly 50 percent of all African American men are listed on the police force's "gang list," even though more than one in three have no criminal record. Being young and Black is guilt enough in capitalist America. Denver, Colorado, is home to another infamous gang list. Until recently, the Denver Police maintained, without public scrutiny, a list of suspected gang members. Because the list was secret, and one only had to be suspected of gang activities to be on it, it was almost impossible to be removed from the list for any reason. Being on the list means you are watched. List information is privy to other police agencies, judges, and could even get out to others, meaning the list could take your job or prejudice a legal case. Two-thirds of all African American youth in Denver were on it as were one in four Latino youth—90 percent of the list was made up of youth of color. A lawsuit forced the police to purge it. But the list still exists.

Libero Della Piana, *Political Affairs*, November 1994.

The dilemma for law enforcement is that while organizations of youths identified as gangs are often connected to criminal activity, the groups are sufficiently disorganized to undermine attempts to apply traditional weapons of police and prosecutors. Although every state has a conspiracy statute and the federal government has the powerful weapons of the Racketeer Influenced and Corrupt Organizations (RICO) and provisions against the Continuing Criminal Enterprise (CCE), the new state and federal efforts developed to attack "gangs" fail to meet the requirements of existing law enforcement tools. The presumption of a shared gang criminal purpose is far from self-evident, and perhaps unprovable.

The moral dimension to the war on gangs does not justify the indiscriminate criminalization of gang membership. If society expects youths to assume responsibility for their actions and conform to social norms despite difficult circumstances, the public must realize that society betrays its youth when it judges and even incarcerates them for the acts of others. The efforts to prosecute gangs and gang members on the basis of social ties is a panic response to a misunderstood crisis; it must stop. . . .

Prosecutorial Definitions of Gangs

Addressing the gang crisis ultimately entails devising a strategy to identify and prosecute gang members. Therefore, it is beneficial to examine anti-gang policy initiatives arising from prosecutors' offices. Sadly, but perhaps predictably, the various definitions are invariably overbroad. These expansive definitions are likely to stigmatize young minority males and exacerbate street crime.

The California Youth Gang Task Force. California is the purported home to one of the nation's most serious gang problems. An advisory group called the California Youth Gang Task Force analyzed the problem and wrestled with the definition of a youth gang. The definition formulated by the California Youth Gang Task Force served as the conceptual focus of its 1988 *Guide for the Investigation and Prosecution of Youth Gang Violence in California.*

Broad Definitions

The California guide established "procedures for conducting investigations of youth gang-related crimes, setting up youth gang files, and conducting the prosecution of youth gang cases." As a matter of "developing a youth gang information file," the guide delineated the following factors as evidence of gang membership:

1. Subject admits being a member of a gang.
2. Subject has tattoos, clothing, etc., that are only associated with certain gangs.
3. Subject has been arrested while participating in activities with a known gang member.
4. Information that places the subject with a gang has been obtained from a reliable informant.
5. Close association with known gang members has been confirmed.

These definitions are notable both for their circuity and potential for abuse. If a law enforcement official determines that one teenager is a gang member and observes the youth with other teens, the official effectively could create a new gang through the straightforward application of the joint participation and "close association" factors. Furthermore, the criteria, even when applied in a restricted fashion, are based upon the presumed convergence of social ties, criminal purpose, and gang identification. Consequently, the application of the criteria could lead to inaccurate determinations that certain youths are members of criminal organizations.

Copying Gang Members

Young children often claim gang membership to achieve status, while older teenagers copy gang symbols from gangs operating in other cities. Clothing and outward symbols of gang consciousness are often unrelated to a criminal purpose; such symbols may in fact be entirely unrelated to gang membership. The close association factor set forth above directly confuses social ties and criminal purpose. As a practical matter, a local teenager may have a difficult time *not* associating with gang members. Close association is only relevant if one can infer a criminal purpose from the association, but social realities demonstrate that this inference is often unwarranted.

Are We All Gang Members?

Gangs were defined on the floor of the Senate in 1993 as a group "that exhibit at least five of the following characteristics: formal membership with required initiation or rules for members; a recognized leader; common clothing, languages, tattoos, turf where the group is known, and a group name." To how many gangs does the reader belong? By this definition, this author belongs to half-a-dozen! And proudly so!

Libero Della Piana, *Political Affairs*, November 1994.

Consider the application of the California criteria to the drug ring chronicled [in *The Cocaine Kids*] by Terry Williams. The drug ring demonstrated a ruthless dedication to the business of selling illegal narcotics. The teenagers, however, carefully concealed their membership in the gang and took other steps to shield their identities unless they felt secure in their social surroundings. Thus, the members of the drug ring would not fit the California guide's gang profile. Yet, pee-wee wannabes would fulfill the guide's definition. Pee wees admit to gang membership, wear gang clothes, and associate with known gang members. Unlike the actual drug ring, the wannabes are unlikely to commit criminal acts or constitute a present danger to the local community. Thus, the California definition does not reliably identify gang members or criminals. . . .

The social forces exposing youngsters to criminals are power-ful. Inner-city homelife and schooling are often inadequate and produce pressures that create social and gang ties independent of criminal purpose. No one, not even the states implementing the anti-gang programs, asserts that increased police surveil-lance and short-term incarceration is the answer to the prob-lems of these young people. Children can be helped by non–law enforcement efforts.

Any policy that puts at-risk youngsters in prison for short peri-ods of time must be considered a spectacular failure. An exam-ple of how the new gang policies and laws could fail is the like-lihood that the use of the anti-gang initiatives will increase the practice of "flipping" [extracting information from] putative gang members. If the police pressure a teenager identified as a gang member to provide information, his attenuated connection with the gang's criminal activity may significantly impair coopera-tion. Accordingly, this younger identified gang member may face criminal penalties for his gang membership while the ac-tual criminals go unpunished. . . .

Individual Responsibility

A return to the principle of individual moral responsibility is a necessary pre-condition to the resolution of the gang problem. The current consensus policy of slightly upgrading the punish-ment for all perceived gang members provides little hope to reform the youngest gang members or free limited resources to incarcerate violent criminals. The young people who commit violent crimes should be punished harshly and removed from so-ciety. However, anti-crime initiatives must deliberately avoid punishing or even "flipping" younger gang members simply be-cause they are perceived as gang members. A special effort should be made to divert less culpable young people from crime through non–law enforcement intervention efforts, even when the youths are involved in criminal activity. Young, non-violent criminals should not be incarcerated, since incarceration will not benefit either the child or society. Law enforcement officials and legislators must recognize that each gang is organized differently and incorporate that understanding of individual gang structures to "flip" actual wrongdoers, invoke conspiracy theories to prose-cute the older ringleaders, and devote available prison resources to the prolonged incarceration of more culpable criminals.

A policy directed toward individual responsibility will have benefits beyond minimizing the harm of wide-spread incarcera-tion of young people. Ironically, treating gangs as dangerous en-emies may encourage gang membership. Treating criminals as individuals, not as members of a gang, could end the common cycle of gang crime and publicity in which massive crackdowns generate publicity and glory for the gang entity. The focus on gangs, as opposed to individuals, tells teenagers as surely as it tells the rest of the public that a particular gang should be feared, respected and admired.

Liberal and Hard-Core Views

When all members of a social group are treated as presumptively culpable, young people have no reason not to admire those who succeed within that framework. Thus, moral messages have a role in structuring American policy toward juvenile offenders, especially since the public concern with gangs arises from a perceived moral breakdown in the inner city. Hard-core anti-gang efforts explicitly, or implicitly, criticize the more liberal social model of gangs [which holds that social and economic conditions are to blame for criminal behavior] as improperly relieving individuals of responsibility for their actions. Yet the anti-gang crusaders assume the same moral position as the apocryphal liberal apologists.

For both the liberal apologists and anti-gang activists, crime results from a moral breakdown in the community. For the apologists, the immorality lies in the conditions that drive young people to crime. This view is not compelling, since not only is individual moral responsibility at the heart of the criminal justice system, but also because youth crime and youth gangs are well entrenched and cannot be explained away as an unhappy coincidence of racism and oppression. For the anti-gang activists, the moral breakdown is the gang itself. This view is even less defensible. Youth groups are not necessarily a crisis, and their extirpation would not be even a symbolic blow at the perceived moral crisis in this country.

Prosecution must be directed at the crime, not the social group. Not only is this the practical solution, but it also is the moral solution. The discomfort and despair of the real world comes early to many inner-city children. The politically expedient war on gangs will bring further pain to those who have done little or nothing to warrant society's wrath and they, once having suffered, will bring further suffering to the rest of us.

"*Juveniles . . . may require an extended correctional placement in training schools, camps, ranches, or other secure options.*"

Convicted Gang Youths May Require Incarceration

John J. Wilson and James C. Howell

Incarceration in youth camps or other secure correctional facilities is a likely outcome for many violent gang youths. In the following viewpoint, John J. Wilson and James C. Howell argue that incarceration must be considered as one method of safeguarding the public from dangerous gang youths and other juvenile offenders. The authors stress that rehabilitation and treatment of such youths must occur in all prevention and incarceration programs. Wilson and Howell are, respectively, deputy administrator and former director of research for the U.S. Department of Justice's Office of Juvenile Justice and Delinquency Prevention in Washington, D.C.

As you read, consider the following questions:

1. How much did juvenile violent crime arrests increase from 1988 to 1992, according to Wilson and Howell?
2. What type of youths do immediate intervention programs target, according to the authors?
3. In the authors' opinion, what should non-community-based treatment programs focus on?

Excerpted from John J. Wilson and James C. Howell, "Serious and Violent Juvenile Crime: A Comprehensive Strategy." Reprinted with permission of the National Council of Juvenile and Family Court Judges, from *Juvenile and Family Court Journal*, vol. 45, no. 2 (Spring 1994).

Serious and violent juvenile crime has increased significantly over the past few years, straining America's juvenile justice system.

Juvenile arrests for violent crimes are increasing. During the period 1983 to 1992, juveniles were responsible for 28% of the increase in murder arrests, 27% of rapes, 27% of robberies, and 17% of aggravated assaults. Most of the increase in violent juvenile crimes during the 10-year period from 1983 to 1992 occurred during the second half of that decade. From 1988 to 1992, juvenile violent crime arrests increased 45%. Increases in juvenile arrests for specific offenses were: murder (52%), rape (17%), robbery (49%), and aggravated assault (47%).

Gang Violence

The national scope and seriousness of the youth gang problem have increased sharply since the early 1980s. Gang violence has risen drastically in a number of large cities. Youth gangs are becoming more violent, and gangs increasingly serve as a way for members to engage in illegal money-making activity, including street-level drug trafficking.

Evidence continues to mount that a small proportion of offenders commit most of the serious and violent juvenile crimes. About 15% of high-risk youth commit about 75% of all violent offenses. Juveniles with four or more court referrals make up 16% of offenders but are responsible for 51% of all juvenile court cases—61% of murder, 64% of rape, 67% of robbery, 61% of aggravated assault, and 66% of burglary cases. . . .

We must identify and control the small group of serious, violent, and chronic juvenile offenders who have committed felony offenses or have failed to respond to intervention and nonsecure community-based treatment and rehabilitation services offered by the juvenile justice system. Measures to address delinquent offenders who are a threat to community safety may include placements in secure community-based facilities or, when necessary, training schools and other secure juvenile facilities. . . .

Graduated Sanctions

An effective juvenile justice system program model for the treatment and rehabilitation of delinquent offenders is one that combines accountability and sanctions with increasingly intensive treatment and rehabilitation services. These graduated sanctions must be wide-ranging to fit the offense and include both intervention and secure corrections components. The intervention component includes the use of immediate intervention and intermediate sanctions, and the secure corrections component includes the use of community confinement and incarceration in training schools, camps, and ranches.

Each of these graduated sanctions components should consist of sublevels, or gradations, that together with appropriate services constitute an integrated approach. The purpose of this approach is to stop the juvenile's further penetration into the system by inducing law-abiding behavior as early as possible through the combination of appropriate intervention and treatment sanctions. The juvenile justice system must work with law enforcement, courts, and corrections to develop reasonable, fair, and humane sanctions.

At each level in the continuum, the family must continue to be integrally involved in treatment and rehabilitation efforts. Aftercare must be a formal component of all residential placements, actively involving the family and the community in supporting and reintegrating the juvenile into the community.

Assessing Risk and Needs

Programs will need to use risk and needs assessments to determine the appropriate placement for the offender. Risk assessments should be based on clearly defined objective criteria that focus on: (1) the seriousness of the delinquent act; (2) the potential risk for re-offending, based on the presence of risk factors; and (3) the risk to the public safety. Effective risk assessment at intake, for example, can be used to identify those juveniles who require the use of detention as well as those who can be released to parental custody or diverted to nonsecure community-based programs. Needs assessments will help ensure that: (1) different types of problems are taken into account when formulating a case plan; (2) a baseline for monitoring a juvenile's progress is established; (3) periodic reassessments of treatment effectiveness are conducted; and (4) a system-wide data base of treatment needs can be used for the planning and evaluation of programs, policies, and procedures. Together, risk and needs assessments will help to allocate scarce resources more efficiently and effectively. A system of graduated sanctions requires a broad continuum of options.

For intervention efforts to be most effective, they must be swift, certain, consistent, and incorporate increasing sanctions, including the possible loss of freedom. As the severity of sanctions increases, so must the intensity of treatment. At each level, offenders must be aware that, should they continue to violate the law, they will be subject to more severe sanctions and could ultimately be confined in a secure setting, ranging from a secure community-based juvenile facility to a training school, camp, or ranch.

The juvenile court plays an important role in the provision of treatment and sanctions. Probation has traditionally been viewed as the court's main vehicle for delivery of treatment services and community supervision. However, traditional probation services and sanctions have not had the resources to effectively target delinquent offenders, particularly serious, violent, and chronic offenders.

Intervention

The following graduated sanctions are proposed within the intervention component:

Immediate intervention. First-time delinquent offenders (misdemeanors and nonviolent felonies) and nonserious repeat offenders (generally misdemeanor repeat offenses) must be targeted for system intervention based on their probability of becoming more serious or chronic in their delinquent activities. Nonresidential community-based programs, including prevention programs for at-risk youth, may be appropriate for many of these offenders. Such programs are small and open, located in or near the juvenile's home, and maintain community participation in program planning, operation, and evaluation. Community police officers, working as part of Neighborhood Resource Teams, can help monitor the juvenile's progress. Other offenders may require sanctions tailored to their offense(s) and their needs to deter them from committing additional crimes.

The following programs apply to these offenders: Neighborhood Resource Teams, diversion, informal probation, school counselors serving as probation officers, home on probation, mediation (victims), community service, restitution, day-treatment programs, alcohol and drug abuse treatment (outpatient), and peer juries.

Intermediate sanctions. Offenders who are inappropriate for immediate intervention (first-time serious or violent offenders) or who fail to respond successfully to immediate intervention as evidenced by re-offending (such as repeat property offenders or drug-involved juveniles) would begin with or be subject to intermediate sanctions. These sanctions may be nonresidential or residential.

Many of the serious and violent offenders at this stage may be appropriate for placement in an intensive supervision program as an alternative to secure incarceration. OJJDP's [Office of Juvenile Justice and Delinquency Prevention] Intensive Supervision of Probationers Program Model is a highly structured, continuously monitored individualized plan that consists of five phases with decreasing levels of restrictiveness: (1) Short-Term Placement in Community Confinement; (2) Day Treatment; (3) Outreach and Tracking; (4) Routine Supervision; and (5) Discharge and Follow-up.

Other appropriate programs include: drug testing, weekend detention, alcohol and drug abuse treatment (inpatient), challenge outdoor [wilderness rehabilitation camps], community-based residential, electronic monitoring, and boot camp facilities and programs.

Public Safety Comes First

While there is much to be said for trying to rehabilitate young offenders, the line must be drawn when a youth commits a violent crime like rape or aggravated assault or murder. In such cases, rehabilitation must take a back seat to public safety.

Maybe while violent young offenders are behind bars, they will, as they say, see the light. Maybe they will commit themselves to treading on the straight and narrow—which certainly should be taken into account when they are eligible for parole. And maybe, ultimately, they will become productive members of society.

But in the here and now, these violent young offenders are a danger to society. They should be given punishments that come much closer to fitting their crimes.

Joseph Perkins, *The Washington Times*, September 11, 1992.

Secure corrections. Large congregate-care juvenile facilities (training schools, camps, and ranches) have not proven to be particularly effective in rehabilitating juvenile offenders. Although some continued use of these types of facilities will remain a necessary alternative for those juveniles who require enhanced security to protect the public, the establishment of small community-based facilities to provide intensive services in a secure environment offers the best hope for successful treatment of those juveniles who require a structured setting. Secure sanctions are most effective in changing future conduct when they are coupled with comprehensive treatment and rehabilitation services.

Standard parole practices, particularly those that have a primary focus on social control, have not been effective in normalizing the behavior of high-risk juvenile parolees over the long term, and consequently, growing interest has developed in intensive aftercare programs that provide high levels of social control and treatment services. OJJDP's Intensive Community-Based Aftercare for High-Risk Juvenile Parolees Program provides an effective aftercare model.

Corrections

The following graduated sanctions strategies are proposed within the secure corrections component:

Community confinement. Offenders whose presenting offense is sufficiently serious (such as a violent felony) or who fail to respond to intermediate sanctions as evidenced by continued reoffending may be appropriate for community confinement. Offenders at this level represent the more serious (such as repeat felony drug trafficking or property offenders) and violent offenders among the juvenile justice system correctional population.

The concept of community confinement provides secure confinement in small community-based facilities that offer intensive treatment and rehabilitation services. These services include individual and group counseling, educational programs, medical services, and intensive staff supervision. Proximity to the community enables direct and regular family involvement with the treatment process as well as a phased re-entry into the community that draws upon community resources and services.

Incarceration in training schools, camps, and ranches. Juveniles whose confinement in the community would constitute an ongoing threat to community safety or who have failed to respond to community-based corrections may require an extended correctional placement in training schools, camps, ranches, or other secure options that are not community based. These facilities should offer comprehensive treatment programs for these youth with a focus on education, skills development, and vocational or employment training and experience. These juveniles may include those convicted in the criminal justice system prior to their reaching the age at which they are no longer subject to the original or extended jurisdiction of the juvenile justice system.

Transfer to the criminal justice system. Public safety concerns are resulting in increasing demands for transfer of the most violent juvenile offenders to the [adult] criminal justice system. These demands will grow as long as American society perceives juveniles to present a disproportionate threat to the public safety. Although state legislatures are increasingly excluding certain categories of juvenile offenders from the jurisdiction of the juvenile court, judicial waiver [to the adult system] holds the most promise as the mechanism for determining that a particular juvenile cannot be rehabilitated in the juvenile justice system. This consideration should be paramount, consistent with the original aims of the juvenile justice system and the juvenile court.

Effective/Promising Programs

Recent reviews of all known experimental evaluations of treatment programs have identified effective program approaches. Interventions that appear to be the most effective include highly structured programs providing intensive treatments over extended periods of time. Juvenile justice system programs that have been effective in treating and rehabilitating serious, violent, and chronic juvenile offenders include intensive supervision programs; day treatment and education programs operated by Associated Marine Institutes (AMI); the Florida Environmental Institute's (FEI) wilderness camp for juveniles who would otherwise be sent to adult prisons; and intensive family-based, multisystemic therapy (MST) programs, which have been effective with serious juvenile offenders in several localities. OJJDP's Violent Juvenile Offender Program demonstrated that most violent juvenile offenders could be successfully rehabilitated through intensive treatment in small secure facilities. OJJDP has also developed an intensive aftercare model designed to successfully reintegrate high-risk juvenile parolees back into the community.

"Prison only reinforces the most inhumane aspects of the streets."

Convicted Gang Youths Should Not Be Incarcerated

Luis J. Rodriguez

Luis J. Rodriguez is an award-winning poet, journalist, and former gang member who writes frequently about Chicano gang youths. In the following viewpoint, Rodriguez contends that incarcerating gang youths is counterproductive. He charges that the criminal justice system and society are prepared to write off an entire generation of Chicano and other gang youths. What these youths need, Rodriguez asserts, are guidance and empowerment.

As you read, consider the following questions:

1. What is the message in Rodriguez's work with young gang members?
2. According to Rodriguez, what is the philosophical basis of capitalism?
3. What are the four aspects of autonomous being, according to the author?

Luis J. Rodriguez, "Writing Off Our Youth," *Prison Life*, October 1994. Reprinted with permission.

In 1993, I entered the guarded gates of the Fred C. Nelles School in Whittier, California—a facility for incarcerated young men ages 10 to 16. Their crimes ranged from incorrigible criminal behavior to murder.

I came to address an assembly of young men dressed in their "blues," many of them members of Los Angeles gangs. The majority at Nelles were Chicano and Latino; the rest were African American. I was introduced as a former gang member and author of the book *Always Running: La Vida Loca, Gang Days in L.A.*

Pain and Pride

On the faces of these wards, some of them marked with tattoos, I saw the pain, the emptiness, the shame and the pride that I felt some 20 years ago when I was part of a barrio, east of Los Angeles.

There, among them, stood defiance and victimization. Honor and inhumanity. Young men and maturing boys.

I spoke to them as honestly as I could, as soft and hard as the occasion required. I'm almost 40 now. An elder perhaps. I haven't been active in the crazy life for decades. But as a teenager, like many of these wards, I sat in jail cells, juvenile courts and alternative schools.

At 18, I barely escaped a long prison term. I had the help of mentors and activists in the most radical wing of the Chicano movement, people to whom I owe my life, people who steered me in the direction of struggle, study and poetic science.

A Message

At Nelles, I didn't preach. I didn't tell the wards what to do. I tried to summarize what I lived to help them assess their own lives: where they've been and where they're going.

I was there to validate their warrior energy, to help them take it to another level of development so they would understand that there's a way to victory, that there's a strategy, there are tactics, there are weapons.

In the intense years of my youth, I fought with guns, knives and fists, subdued by spray intoxicants, pills and heroin. Today I fight with words, ideas and poetry. I'm still a warrior, but now with weapons that have proven more effective and powerful than any gun I held in my hand.

The wards took in what I said. Some were silent, which is also a way of communicating. They appeared to be thinking, perhaps feeling again. A few questions came my way. But much of the time called for contemplation.

At the end, a 16-year-old Chicano came up to me and shook my hand. "I've never been as proud of being a Mexican as when I heard you speak here today," he said.

I could already see he was on a transcendent path, that he was tapping into the transformative powers within him. Then I asked the dude why he was *torcido* [incarcerated].

"For two murders and eleven murder attempts."

Billions Spent, No Return

Society's anger at [gang members] has resulted in longer prison sentences and harsher laws. But there's not enough space to warehouse them all, and there never will be, so they are let out, with few resources for being successful in the world outside their gang.

It's strange that we are so willing to spend billions of dollars in tax money imprisoning young men, but we don't get anything in return except another trip back to prison for them. Seems like a waste of money, and a waste of young men in their prime of life.

Jim Gogek, *The San Diego Union-Tribune*, April 26, 1993.

As far as the criminal justice system is concerned, this young man was not going anywhere. But I sensed he was already on a new journey of discovery, empowerment and social clarification.

This is the message in my work: that change is possible, that it is necessary. And most importantly, that everyone can be their own agents of change, can transcend even the worst experiences.

A Double Standard

This society, as personified in its prison system, is saying the exact opposite. If you're poor, if you're of color, or an immigrant, you can never change. You are born with a brand of mediocrity, of mind enslavement, of no options.

This is reinforced by a strangling double standard of justice, where certain laws and social norms do not apply to the rich or resourceful.

On the one hand, if a member of this society's ruling class does wrong, it is automatic they will have options to do better. But for those of us without the means, we are given "jackets" to wear for life.

The "three strikes and you're out" concept is not new; it only institutionalizes what has been happening to a particular segment of the population for years.

Prison only reinforces the most inhumane aspects of the streets. It is internalized colonialism and oppression. The "criminal" justice system operates on the deepest and most pervasive level of inhumanity.

This is why "respect" is a life-and-death issue in prisons. When it has been denied, when people are torn down by the most degrading treatment, they try to hang on to respect as the one last thing of value.

For the last few years, I've facilitated poetry workshops in prisons, homeless shelters and migrant camps. I've emphasized the liberating aspects of poetic expression. It involves relating to the intrinsic value we have as human beings. Poetry is about connecting again to feelings, to other human beings with language, meaning and music.

This is why raw artistic expression, often in language, is found among those who have been most marginalized in society. When one's being has been devalued, one reaches into the depths of creativity and imagination and brings it out again: hot, searing and unconquerable.

Capitalist Society

But the capitalist society, unable to accommodate most of this next generation, is prepared to write them off. The strategy is to first criminalize them, to distance them from "civil" society (even though this society is uncivilized at its core).

Although I have avoided a prison term for 20 years, I am still within the prison parameters, being from the barrio, a Chicano and a poet. My work behind the walls, in the shelters and the boys' homes is to assist our collective efforts against all the barriers, to remove the imposed sentencing without due process given to us because of our station in life.

Capitalism is not an ideology. It's an economic system. But it has an underlying philosophical basis: pragmatism, to do what is expedient, of getting over [succeeding], the only thing that matters is results (profits). Competition drives the system; dog-eat-dog. Only the strong (in reality, the privileged) survive.

This philosophy permeates the streets and jails, where the one who gets over is the one who cares the least. Where did we learn this, if not from our social relations?

You think those who rule this country, who are often the first ones to propose "three strikes and you're out," "zero tolerance" and similar measures are above moral degeneration? Or blackmail? Or theft or murder?

Think again.

Look at the revelations of [longtime FBI chief] J. Edgar Hoover (who blackmailed, lied and perhaps murdered to maintain his power through seven presidents) or the way that perpetual victim Oliver North ran for Virginia senator, knowing he does not have to pay for what he has done. [North's 1989 conviction for obstructing Congress after coordinating the Iran-Contra arms-for-hostages operation was overturned and the case dismissed in

1991.] Or how Los Angeles police officer Stacey Koon [convicted in 1993 for beating black motorist Rodney King] and billionaire bonds crook Michael Milken [imprisoned for twenty-two months for securities fraud] are totally devoid of remorse.

There are people in this society who not only feel empowered—they feel entitled. They know they will ultimately rule without consent. They know they will obtain wealth and power no matter what the immediate costs or consequences.

Chicano Empowerment

As a Chicano, born into this world stripped of dignity, history and culture, bereft of my language and land, how will I respond? *Mi Vida Loca* [a film about Chicana gang members] was a response. Tattoos on our faces, our arms, our backs—the inside wounds on the body were a response. For this we may be condemned, but this was our stand. This is how we negotiated our identity outside of true power.

Now we have to make our own history. We have to prepare our youth to be sovereign over their lives, their community, their country. To be rulers, lovers, artists and warriors (the four aspects of autonomous being).

This is why I believe in that 16-year-old Nelles warrior. There are millions like him. They are seeking the eldership and revolutionary skills to struggle, to think, to triumph.

We, who have already forged through this, must guide these young people through the journey they honor with their presence. No more prisons. No more mediocrity. No more slavery. It's time for us to rule.

"*The nuisance abatement strategy . . . is both unsound as a policy matter and constitutionally infirm.*"

Gang Antiloitering Laws Are Unconstitutional

Terence R. Boga

In recent years, local governments have begun invoking nuisance abatement laws in an attempt to curb gang activity. In the following viewpoint, Terence R. Boga argues that these antiloitering laws are misguided and unconstitutional. Boga contends that the U.S. Supreme Court has long recognized that the freedom of assembly protects people who have engaged in past illegal activity. He asserts that while unlawful gang activity should be prosecuted, gang members have the right to peaceful public assembly. Boga is a graduate of Harvard Law School in Cambridge, Massachusetts, and an attorney specializing in municipal law in Los Angeles, California.

As you read, consider the following questions:

1. What type of conduct did the Los Angeles civil lawsuit against the Playboy Gangster Crips seek to prohibit, according to Boga?
2. According to the author, why did a court strike down the East Lansing, Michigan, "safety zones" ordinance?
3. Why are increases in arrests and incarceration the wrong approach against gangs, in Boga's opinion?

From Terence R. Boga, "Turf Wars: Street Gangs, Local Governments, and the Battle for Public Space," *Harvard Civil Rights-Civil Liberties Law Review*, vol. 29, no. 2 (Summer 1994), pages 477-502. Reprinted with permission granted by the *Harvard Civil Rights-Civil Liberties Law Review*, ©1994 by the President and Fellows of Harvard College.

In cities across America, public streets have become contested ground in territorial struggles among urban gangs. Tragically, gang violence has escalated to the point of ubiquity, resulting in the mutilation and death of countless participants and innocent bystanders. Though seemingly purposeless, these turf wars are often propelled by the desire to control lucrative drug markets and by a neighborhood-centered jingoism. While the criminal justice system has made significant accommodations to facilitate the arrest and prosecution of delinquent gang members, there is growing sentiment that new law enforcement techniques are necessary to stymie the mounting urban disorder.

In California, local governments are waging a turf war of their own by means of an innovative prosecutorial gambit. Municipalities are increasingly pressing courts to deploy their nuisance abatement power against street gangs. Judges have responded with sweeping injunctions restraining gang members from fighting, possessing weapons, spraying graffiti, and trespassing on private property. More alarmingly, courts have also commanded gang members not to congregate together publicly. Through the magic of a judicial order, even purely social association becomes a punishable offense, subjecting violators to months of incarceration and significant fines. By means of this civil remedy, cities are effectively banishing street gangs from the realm of public space. . . .

The Abatement of Street Gangs

After a tentative beginning, the deployment of the nuisance abatement power against street gangs has proceeded with astonishing speed. Over a matter of months, California municipalities bombarded courts with lists of "gang activity" too offensive to be tolerated. Judges, convinced of the asserted inadequacy of criminal law strategies, imposed severe restrictions on the liberties of all members of targeted gangs. Although the particulars varied, abatement orders uniformly forbade youths from gathering on public streets for any purpose, without an individualized determination of delinquency.

On October 26, 1987, Los Angeles City Attorney James Hahn opened a new chapter in legal history by filing a nuisance abatement lawsuit against an urban street gang. The civil suit, *People v. Playboy Gangster Crips*, asked the court to issue a twenty-three-point injunction against the two hundred–plus gang members prohibiting a broad range of legal and illicit conduct including: wearing gang colors; associating with other gang members; possessing firearms, paint, or markers; remaining in public longer than five minutes; and leaving their residences after nightfall. Only through collective liability, prosecutors maintained, could law enforcement cope with a criminal enterprise

133

that was organized to the level of posting sentries with walkie-talkies on street corners to warn drug dealers of approaching police officers.

Los Angeles Superior Court Judge Warren Deering deemed the City's request for a temporary restraining order (TRO) too broad to grant on an *ex parte* [for the sake of one party only] basis. Attempting to accommodate criticism by civil libertarians, Hahn subsequently modified the complaint by limiting the curfew to minors, restricting the ban on association to public gatherings, and eliminating the prohibition on wearing gang attire. Despite these concessions, Judge Deering ultimately granted just six of the City's requests in an order that generally forbade activities that were already crimes. Still, municipalities besieged by gang violence and drug dealing could consider the lawsuit a success, for it signaled a new addition to the law enforcement arsenal. . . .

In October 1992, Burbank became the second California city to apply the law of public nuisance to street gangs. In *People ex rel. Fletcher v. Acosta*, prosecutors won an injunction that banned eighty-eight suspected members of the Barrio Elmwood Rifa gang from congregating publicly and from performing a variety of illegal activities on the 100 block of West Elmwood Avenue. The prohibited zone, the center of the city's highest crime area, was the site of fifty-seven percent of the reported gunfire incidents during the year. Comparing the gang members to the Brown Shirts of Nazi Germany, Burbank Superior Court Judge Thomas Murphy declared: "These guys can't just say it's their turf. That turf is the city of Burbank, the state of California and United States of America. They have no right to terrorize people there."

"No Turf Is Gang Turf"

Inspired by this success, Los Angeles again deployed the new-found weapon four months later. City Attorney Hahn echoed Judge Murphy's characterization of a battle between municipalities and street gangs for control of public space: "They think it's their turf, and we want to send out the real strong message that no turf is gang turf in this city." In *People v. Blythe Street Gang*, Van Nuys Superior Court Judge John Major issued a preliminary injunction against the 350-member gang granting virtually all of the City's requests. Explaining his imposition of collective liability, Judge Major observed: "The Blythe Street Gang shares common purposes to recruit new members, to control the . . . area as their 'turf' and to engage in activities designed to further their reign of terror." The unprecedented breadth of the injunction, both in terms of geography and the numerical size of the affected class, inspired some supporters of previous uses of the civil remedy to reconsider their position. . . .

Finally, the Orange County city of Westminster enjoyed a

short-lived victory over the West Trece gang in a legal battle to control the gang's presence in a twenty-five-square-block neighborhood. In July 1993, prosecutors obtained a temporary restraining order in *People ex. rel. Jones v. Amaya* prohibiting fifty-nine gang members from meeting together in public and from violating various weapons, property defacement, and trespass laws. The civil order remained in effect for two months before Orange County Superior Court Judge Richard Beacom terminated the ban in a ruling denying the City's application for a preliminary injunction. Although branding the West Trece gang a "terrorist organization" and warning that "we're on the edge of anarchy," Judge Beacom declared that traditional principles of equitable discretion, as well as protection of the state and federal constitutions, precluded the City's tactic.

An Unjust Ban

If gang members can be banned from a public park, why not ban convicted freeway shooters or convicted repeat-drunk drivers from public highways, or ban convicted robbers from all twenty-four-hour convenience stores and so on?

Alexander A. Molina, *Southwestern University Law Review*, Winter 1993.

Of the nuisance lawsuits against street gangs thus far, the Westminster action was the first to be struck down. To date, there have been no higher court decisions concerning the validity of the civil strategy, although tests are pending. Within two months of Judge Beacom's ruling, Westminster prosecutors appealed the decision, characterizing it as an improper balancing of the rights of citizens against the rights of gang members. In late August 1993, reputed Blythe Street gang member Jessie Gonzalez became the first person convicted of violating an abatement order. His infractions included possessing a pager and a glass bottle, trespassing, and obstructing traffic. Gonzalez was sentenced to ninety days in jail and given three years probation. The Los Angeles County public defender's office is challenging the conviction as well as the underlying court order.

In those communities where an abatement injunction has been in effect, authorities consider it an unqualified success. Law enforcement officers reported a total cessation of gang incidents in the 100 block of West Elmwood Avenue six months after Burbank's *Acosta* injunction was issued. Orange County prosecutors reported a similar drop in gang activity for the two-month period that Westminster's *Amaya* TRO was in force. Whether these court orders actually reduce the incidence of criminal gang activity or merely displace it to other neighborhoods is unclear. Nonetheless, the apparent effectiveness of the civil remedy has already inspired the City of Norwalk to announce its intention to file a nuisance suit of its own. Should the *Blythe Street Gang* and *Amaya* injunctions be upheld on appeal [the cases were pending as of March 1995], it is not unreasonable to expect the widespread abatement of street gangs throughout California. . . .

Peaceable Assembly

Abatement injunction prohibitions on public congregation implicate the First Amendment freedom of peaceable assembly. Although often conflated with the right of association by prior analysts, the assembly liberty actually presents a separate constitutional hurdle to local government efforts at dispersing street gangs. While the [U.S.] Supreme Court has effectively closed the door on social association arguments, several cases leave open the possibility that social assembly is protected. Even if a right to social assembly is not recognized, bans on public congregation must fail under the overbreadth doctrine for deterring clearly protected activities.

The 1971 case of *Coates v. Cincinnati* intimates the possible scope of the Assembly Clause. There, the Court held that a municipal ordinance that made it a crime for three or more persons to gather on a sidewalk "and there conduct themselves in a manner annoying to passers by" violated both the vagueness element of the Due Process Clause [of the Fourteenth Amendment regarding due process of law] and the rights of free assembly and association. Significantly, the Court's decision was made without knowledge of the details of the appellants' conduct. That the ordinance permitted "the right of the people to gather in public places for *social* and political purposes" to be suspended on the basis of "mere public intolerance or animosity" justified its invalidation regardless of the particular conduct at hand.

The language of *Coates* is broad enough to suggest that the First Amendment protection of peaceable assembly extends to purely social gatherings. The facts of the case, however, render such an expansive interpretation questionable. The appellants in *Coates* were a student involved in a demonstration and two picketers involved in a labor dispute; whatever the nature of their conduct, it does not seem likely that it was nonexpressive. Similarly, one has to be skeptical of this subsequent declaration by a three-Justice plurality: "People assemble in public places not only to speak or to take action, but also to listen, observe, and learn; indeed, they may 'assembl[e] for any lawful purpose.'" This dicta was announced in the course of a decision to grant the public and the media a right of access to a criminal trial. In fact, it has often been the case that the Court's most grandiose statements concerning the breadth of the right of assembly in public fora have been made in situations where some other First Amendment right was being exercised.

Rights of Suspected Criminals

Whatever the precise boundaries of the assembly right, it is long settled that the freedom of assembly may not be curbed on the grounds that some of the participants have engaged in illegal activity at other times. The Court addressed the assembly rights of suspected criminals in 1936 in *De Jonge v. Oregon*. There, Dirk De Jonge appealed a seven-year sentence imposed for assisting in the conduct of a meeting sponsored by the Communist Party. A unanimous Court reversed his conviction and held that peaceable assembly for lawful political discussion cannot be made a crime. It reasoned that states are free to protect themselves against misuse of the assembly right by means of laws targeting the abuse:

> If the persons assembling have committed crimes elsewhere, if they have formed or are engaged in a conspiracy against the public peace and order, they may be prosecuted for their conspiracy or other violation of valid laws. But it is a different matter when the State, instead of prosecuting them for such offenses, seizes upon mere participation in a peaceable assembly and a lawful public discussion as the basis for a criminal charge.

Nuisance abatement orders preventing gang members from congregating publicly operate on this same faulty principle. Rather than apply existing laws to punish illicit gatherings, they seek to criminalize all meetings by gang members regardless of the motivation.

While gang members do not regularly meet for political purposes, the public congregation provision of nuisance abatement injunctions threatens their exercise of the right to peaceable assembly. Government regulations that, in the course of criminalizing unprotected activity, effectively deter constitutionally protected conduct are void under the overbreadth doctrine. In answer to the question of how wide the state can cast its net, the Court has declared in *Broaderick v. Oklahoma*: "the overbreadth of a statute must not only be real, but substantial as well, judged in relation to the statute's plainly legitimate sweep." The plainly legitimate sweep of an abatement order covers disorderly conduct and organized drug dealing on public streets. Yet public congregation provisions reach much further than this and have the potential to subject targeted gang members to contempt proceedings for simply attending a rally against police brutality.

Local government prohibitions on public association satisfy

the substantiality requirement of the overbreadth doctrine. In a case analogous to the gang abatement scenario, the Michigan city of East Lansing attempted to prevent vandalism and property destruction by raucous participants of a semi-annual college street party by banning all student assemblies. A local ordinance empowered the mayor to declare entire neighborhoods "safety zones" and exclude nonresidents from entering or gathering based on an anticipated disturbance or emergency. The Sixth Circuit ruled the law unconstitutional. "Although we recognize the compelling interest which the [City] has in abating the public nuisance created by Cedarfest, we believe that there are more appropriate methods than adopting an ordinance which also permits the city to prevent the occurrence of events which enjoy constitutional protection."

The Right to Associate

An individual still has the right to associate with another even though the latter may conduct unlawful activities. Mere association with criminals does not necessarily mean promoting or assisting in unlawful acts. . . . People have the right to associate with whomever they please, even criminals. But, although one's right to free association is not absolute, any limitations upon it are subject to strict scrutiny.

Alexander A. Molina, *Southwestern University Law Review*, Winter 1993.

There is no concrete difference between East Lansing's ordinance and the nuisance abatement orders employed by California municipalities. They share both the goal of preventing delinquent public conduct and the effect of impeding lawful social assembly. In Michigan, at least, this strategy is impermissible.

Local governments are understandably concerned about soaring rates of gang violence and drug dealing. The nuisance abatement strategy developed by California municipalities, however, is both unsound as a policy matter and constitutionally infirm. Effective law enforcement can and should be conducted in a manner that preserves gang members' access to public space for recreational and social purposes.

Unlawful gang activity should, of course, be punished. Cities have a variety of criminal law measures with which to control delinquent behavior. Yet, in the long run, reliance on increased arrest and incarceration will merely slow the tide of urban disorder. No matter how stringent the law enforcement procedure, it will be compromised both because gangs and police develop informal rules of interaction, and because prisons merely reproduce gangs in a different forum. Thus, intervention techniques are needed to prevent the next generation from becoming engaged in illicit conduct.

Youth Alternatives

Adolescents migrate to street gangs because their desires for community, power, and money are not being met elsewhere. In order to achieve significant progress against urban violence, society must provide legitimate alternatives that satisfy these basic needs. Many municipalities have begun experimenting with different methods of doing just that. In conjunction with representatives of the private sector, Cleveland created a college scholarship program for students in grades seven through twelve that credits their account for good grades earned. Other cities are instituting community clubs to lure youths off the streets. These are excellent models. The most serious mistake society can make is to give up on gang members. Elected officials, law enforcement personnel, and the public at large would do well to consider the words of [writer and former gang member] Luis Rodriguez:

> Gangs are not alien powers. They begin as unstructured groupings, our children, who desire the same as any young person. Respect. A sense of belonging. Protection. The same thing that the YMCA, Little League or the Boy Scouts want. It wasn't any more than what I wanted as a child.
>
> Gangs flourish when there's a lack of social recreation, decent education or employment. Today, many young people will never know what it is to work. They can only satisfy their needs through collective strength—against the police, who hold the power of life and death, against poverty, against idleness, against their impotence in society.

"Regarding the dangers and intimidation caused by criminal street gangs, the prohibition of loitering by these persons is reasonable."

Gang Antiloitering Laws Can Be Made Constitutional

Lisa A. Kainec

In the following viewpoint, Lisa A. Kainec highlights the validity of a 1992 Chicago antiloitering ordinance designed to prevent criminal gang activities such as murder, robbery, and burglary. Kainec acknowledges that while antiloitering ordinances can raise doubts of constitutionality, the Chicago measure's addition of a dispersement clause—declaring it a violation for suspected gang members to disobey a police officer's order to disperse—makes the ordinance constitutional. Kainec maintains that Chicago and other gang-ridden cities need this type of ordinance to protect citizens and their communities. Kainec, an attorney in Cleveland, wrote this viewpoint as a law student at Case Western Reserve University in Cleveland.

As you read, consider the following questions:

1. According to Kainec, why must the Chicago ordinance pass a "more stringent vagueness test"?
2. Why will the ordinance not be subject to arbitrary enforcement, in Kainec's opinion?
3. How does the ordinance treat loiterers who are not gang members, according to the author?

Excerpted from Lisa A. Kainec, "Curbing Gang-Related Violence in America: Do Gang Members Have a Constitutional Right to Loiter on Our Streets?" *Case Western Reserve Law Review*, vol. 43, no. 2 (Winter 1993). Reprinted with permission, including permission to delete the footnotes that appear in the original.

Public officials today are faced with ever increasing crime rates and escalating violence in their cities and on their streets. Many people attribute these urban disasters to the rise of gang and drug activity. Lawmakers' efforts have been on-going in recent years to curb such violence, resulting in the enactment of many laws aimed at crime prevention. On June 17, 1992, the City of Chicago passed an ordinance that allows police to order persons reasonably believed to be gang members who are observed loitering on the City's streets to disperse. Failure to obey the order is a violation of the ordinance for which the loiterer may be arrested.

Chicago's ordinance is expected to be challenged on constitutional grounds. Loitering laws have faced constitutional challenges on several occasions, the central concern being the potential for abuse and arbitrary enforcement. Whether Chicago's ordinance can quell this fear of misuse of power and meet the strict constitutional criteria that protect conduct considered innocent will decide the fate of this attempt by a City to protect its citizens. . . .

This comment argues that Chicago's ordinance should pass constitutional muster and be upheld as a legitimate and appropriate means by which to combat the problems of escalating violence and crime in American cities. . . .

The Chicago City Ordinance

In enacting its new ordinance, the City Council of Chicago made several legislative findings indicative of the Council's purpose and objectives. Specifically, the Council found that Chicago's murder rate and rate of violent and drug-related crimes have been increasing, a phenomenon experienced by many other U.S. cities. The Council further found that the increase in criminal street gang activity has been largely responsible for the situation and that the law-abiding citizens of Chicago have been intimidated by the presence of street gang members in public places.

Street gangs establish control over identifiable areas of the City by loitering in those areas, intimidating others from entering such areas. Further, the Council stated that gang members avoid arrest by committing no offense punishable under existing law, but maintain control over identifiable areas by continued loitering; this loitering creates a justifiable fear for the safety of persons and property because of the violent activity often associated with criminal street gangs. The City has a legitimate interest in discouraging all persons from loitering with criminal gang members. As a consequence, the Council resolved to take the aggressive action necessary "to preserve the City's streets and other public places so that the public may use such places without fear."

The ordinance provides:

(a) Whenever a police officer observes a person whom he reasonably believes to be a criminal street gang member loitering in any public place with one or more other persons, he shall order all such persons to disperse and remove themselves from the area. Any person who does not promptly obey such an order is in violation of this section.

(b) It shall be an affirmative defense to an alleged violation of this section that no person who was observed loitering was in fact a member of a criminal street gang.

(c) As used in this Section:

(1) "Loiter" means to remain in any one place with no apparent purpose.

(2) "Criminal street gang" means any ongoing organization, association in fact or group of three or more persons, whether formal or informal, having as one of its substantial activities the commission of one or more of the criminal acts enumerated in paragraph (3), and whose members individually or collectively engage in or have engaged in a pattern of criminal gang activity.

(3) "Criminal gang activity" means the commission, attempted commission, or solicitation of offenses, provided that the offenses are committed by two or more persons, or by an individual at the direction of, or in association with, any criminal street gang, with the specific intent to promote, further, or assist in any criminal conduct by gang members[.]

(4) "Pattern of criminal gang activity" means two or more acts of criminal gang activity of which at least two such acts were committed within five years of each other and at least one such act occurred after the effective date of this Section.

(5) "Public place" means the public way and any other location open to the public, whether publicly or privately owned.

(d) Any person who violates this Section is subject to a fine of not less than $100 and not more than $500 for each offense, or imprisonment for not more than six months, or both.

In addition to or instead of the above penalties, any person who violates this Section may be required to perform up to 120 hours of community service.

Reasonable Exercise of Police Power?

As the United States Supreme Court has recognized, a "city is free to prevent people from blocking sidewalks, obstructing traffic, littering streets, committing assaults, or engaging in countless other forms of antisocial conduct." States have the right to exercise police powers in order to protect the health and safety of their citizens and the morals of the community. Accordingly, the existence of loitering and vagrancy statutes is commonly justified based on the threat of future criminality to the public well-being.

So long as legislation has a real and substantial relation to the ends sought to be achieved and is not "arbitrary, discriminatory, capricious or unreasonable," it will not infringe upon the Constitution. However, where such legislation places restrictions on individual freedom of action as an exercise of police power, those restrictions must be reasonably related to the public good to be upheld as constitutional.

Strict Constitutional Requirements

Laws [against loitering or drug-related activity] must (1) apprise the public of the specific conduct that is prohibited such that a person of ordinary intelligence may behave accordingly; (2) establish minimum guidelines to govern the enforcement of the law such that it may not be enforced in an arbitrary or erratic manner; and (3) define the prohibited conduct in sufficiently specific terms to ensure that constitutionally protected conduct is not brought within its sweep.

Lisa A. Kainec, *Case Western Reserve Law Review*, Winter 1993.

Based on the legislative findings of the City Council set forth in the Chicago Ordinance's preamble, it is apparent that the Council is addressing a matter of grave concern to it and the citizens of Chicago. The Council stated that "intimidation by gang members who gather in public places has made many residents virtual prisoners in their own homes." Indeed, the life of the community is threatened when groups such as gangs and drug dealers dominate the streets for their illegal purposes. Moreover, while people have a constitutional right to associate with others, including the right to assemble in public, no individual or group of individuals has a constitutional right to assemble on public property for illegal activity. Thus, it would appear that Chicago's prohibition against gang members' loitering on public streets is reasonably related to the ends of furthering public safety and protecting the community.

Void for Vagueness?

The vagueness doctrine requires that the Ordinance both provide notice to the public of the prohibited conduct and establish minimum guidelines to guard against arbitrary enforcement of its terms. Moreover, since this Ordinance is aimed at loitering, an activity held to be constitutionally protected by the United States Supreme Court, the law must pass a more stringent vagueness test because of the threat that a constitutionally protected activity may be inhibited.

Applying the first prong of the vagueness test—the notice requirement—the Ordinance must meet the ordinary intelligence test. It must "give a person of ordinary intelligence fair notice that his contemplated conduct is forbidden by the statute." The Chicago Ordinance prohibits loitering by criminal street gang members with one or more other persons in any public place.

This prohibition alone would be insufficient to notify even the narrowly defined class of "criminal street gang members" of the conduct prohibited. Because loitering is defined in the Ordinance as "[remaining] in any one place with no apparent purpose," such behavior still falls within the definition of protected conduct set forth by the Supreme Court. In addition, the prohibition alone is inadequate to notify a person who may unknowingly loiter with a gang member that his or her conduct is prohibited.

However, these infirmities may be overcome by the Ordinance's addition of the dispersement requirement. Before any person can be deemed to have violated the Ordinance, that person must in fact have been observed loitering with a criminal street gang and thereafter refuse to obey the order of the observing police officer to disperse. With this additional requirement, the Ordinance no longer prohibits mere loitering; rather, it prohibits loitering *plus* some additional act. Because of the overt act requirement—refusal to disperse—the public is adequately informed of the prohibited conduct. Mere loitering is insufficient to establish a violation. Additionally, disobedience of a police order is required.

This dispersement requirement also serves to cure the Ordinance of the vagueness of the term "known gang member." The Ordinance permits the police to order dispersement of persons loitering with an individual the officer "reasonably believes to be a criminal street gang member." The determination of whether a loiterer is a criminal street gang member under this standard is obviously left to the subjective judgment of the police officer. "It is a long-accepted principle that the mere status of an individual cannot be made criminal." If the officer's subjective belief regarding the status of the individual were enough to establish a violation of this criminal ordinance, the ordinance would surely fail for vagueness. There would be no way to ascertain to whom the ordinance would apply because the standard is at best unclear.

Nevertheless, the Ordinance in fact should not fail for vagueness because more than the officer's subjective determination is required to establish a violation. The alleged gang member and others observed loitering must refuse to disperse, which, as discussed above, is an overt act that must occur prior to arrest. The dispersement requirement also serves as a means by which persons who may not themselves be gang members, but who loiter with another who may be a gang member unbeknownst to them, may avoid criminal punishment. By dispersing upon order, that person avoids any adverse consequences whether or not he or she knew the other loiterer was a gang member. Therefore, the Ordinance passes the first prong of the vagueness test by defining in precise terms the conduct that is prohibited.

Additionally, the dispersement requirement arguably brings the Ordinance within the second prong of the vagueness test, which requires the establishment of standards sufficient to prevent ad hoc or arbitrary enforcement. This second prong requires that the Ordinance establish minimum guidelines by which law enforcement officials can determine whether and when a violation has occurred. The purpose of these guidelines is to guard against subjective and arbitrary enforcement of the Ordinance at the whim of police or other prosecuting officials.

Were the Chicago Ordinance merely to prohibit "loitering for no apparent purpose," the determination of whether an individual had manifested any "purpose" would be left strictly to the subjective judgment of the law enforcement official. This problem has been overcome in many loitering statutes by the requirement that prior to arrest, an individual manifest a particular purpose or specific intent to engage in criminal activity in order to establish a violation. In many cases, this purpose or intent has been inferred from the observance of several behaviors enumerated in the particular statute or ordinance.

The Chicago Ordinance, however, does not follow this pattern. Instead of requiring the observance of several overt acts from which intent may be inferred, this Ordinance requires one specific overt act to establish a violation. Specifically, the persons observed loitering with a known gang member will be ordered to disperse by police. It is only if and when these persons refuse to obey the police order that they will have violated the Ordinance.

Since loitering itself is an overt act, the police will be able to observe this behavior if it occurs once their order to disperse has been made. Therefore, because overt behavior must be observed in order to establish a violation following a police order to disperse, this Ordinance will not be subject to arbitrary enforcement based upon the subjective judgment of the enforcement officials. Until refusal to disperse has been manifested by continued loitering, no violation has occurred, and no one may be arrested under the Ordinance.

Unconstitutionally Overbroad?

The Ordinance will be constitutionally void if it prohibits constitutionally protected activity. While loitering generally is protected conduct, the loitering described and prohibited by the

Chicago Ordinance is of a narrow class. Only loitering by or with a known gang member is prohibited. Given the City Council's findings regarding the dangers and intimidation caused by criminal street gangs, the prohibition of loitering by these persons is reasonable in light of the ends sought to be achieved.

While gang members and persons who may loiter with them in public do indeed have the rights of assembly and association as does any other citizen, "no individual or group of individuals has a right to gather for an illegal activity." The Chicago Ordinance defines criminal street gangs as having criminal activity as one of their substantial activities. It is reasonable, therefore, for the City Council to believe that loitering by or with gang members on public streets may constitute the use of public property for the furtherance of gang activity.

However, neither a person's status nor his or her "propensity" to commit crime may be the proper basis for arresting a person observed loitering. An ordinance that "effectively transforms into criminal behavior ordinary conduct of individuals on the basis of . . . status . . . is patently unconstitutional." The status of a loiterer as a gang member, however, is not the element upon which a violation of the ordinance turns. The individual's status makes reasonable the requirement that the loiterers disperse, but the refusal to disperse is the actual violation.

Moreover, the statute provides an affirmative defense to an alleged violation of the Ordinance where no person observed loitering is in fact a member of a criminal street gang. In the event a police officer mistakenly, or even willfully, arrests a person for loitering who was not loitering with a criminal gang member, that person could not be punished. Such an arrest "would not be a proper application of the ordinance, and the fact that a law may be improperly applied or even abused does not render it constitutionally invalid." When properly applied, the Chicago Ordinance does not bring within its sweep constitutionally protected conduct—it merely prohibits loitering activity to the extent necessary to achieve the City's legitimate and reasonable objectives of reducing crime and ensuring the continued viability of its neighborhoods.

The Chicago gang loitering ordinance represents a novel approach to the growing crime and violence of America's inner cities. The ability to prohibit conduct before any criminal activity has taken place has been sought by the enactment of numerous loitering laws in the past. Strong constitutional protections, however, have thwarted the efforts of cities and states to attain such power.

While the Chicago Ordinance will no doubt soon be challenged in the courts as an unconstitutional infringement on individuals' rights, the Ordinance should not fail for constitutional vagueness or overbreadth. If the Ordinance is nevertheless struck down, perhaps we as Americans should begin to ask ourselves if the protection of individual constitutional rights should at some point be subordinated to the protection of our cities and communities. For if the communities we call "home" are destroyed, the America that the Constitution is meant to protect and preserve may well cease to exist.

Periodical Bibliography

The following articles have been selected to supplement the diverse views presented in this chapter.

Associated Press
"Teachers Union Proposes Expelling Students Who Assault Others or Carry in Guns or Drugs," *The New York Times*, July 19, 1994.

Neela Banerjee
"Curfews Spread, but Effects Are Still Not Clear," *The Wall Street Journal*, March 4, 1994.

David Chanoff
"James Galipeau, Street Redeemer," *The New York Times Magazine*, November 13, 1994.

CQ Researcher
"Juvenile Justice: Should Violent Youths Get Tougher Punishments?" February 25, 1994. Available from 1414 22nd St. NW, Washington, DC 20037.

Edwin J. Delattre
"Pushing Against Our Age," *The American School Board Journal*, July 1994. Available from 1680 Duke St., Alexandria, VA 22314.

Amitai Etzioni
"How Our Towns Fight Crime," *The Wall Street Journal*, December 31, 1993.

Harvard Law Review
"Juvenile Curfews and Gang Violence: Exiled on Main Street," May 1994.

Mike Males
"Willie Horton Jr.," *In These Times*, December 27, 1993.

Eugene H. Methvin
"When the Gangs Came to Tacoma," *Reader's Digest*, May 1992.

Alexander A. Molina
"California's Anti-Gang Street Terrorism Enforcement and Prevention Act: One Step Forward, Two Steps Back?" *Southwestern University Law Review*, Winter 1993.

The New Yorker
"Ganging Up on the Gangs," October 10, 1994.

Lee Ranck
"Gangs with a Vision of Peace," *Christian Social Action*, June 1993. Available from 100 Maryland Ave. NE, Washington, DC 20002.

Luis J. Rodriguez
"Turning Youth Gangs Around," *The Nation*, November 21, 1994.

Ronald D. Stephens
"Gangs, Guns, and School Violence," *USA Today*, January 1994.

Personal Narratives: How Do Gang Members View Themselves?

Chapter Preface

Many news stories and features about gangs cite the opinions of police officers, criminologists, sociologists, and others regarding the gang phenomenon. Often lacking in such reports, however, are the views of gang members themselves, perhaps because of their secrecy or distrust of the media.

Personal testimony from gang members can provide valuable insight into gangs and the gang culture. "You have to understand their world to know what's important to them," says Marianne Diaz-Parton, a former gang member who now directs a Los Angeles gang outreach program. "There's a reason behind every gang member that's out there."

In the following chapter, gang members describe common yet diverse experiences—admitting to brutal acts of violence, justifying their lifestyle, and explaining what they gained or lost from their gang involvement.

"I can't believe I was willing to die for a [gang] color, a damn meaningless color."

The Gang Life Is a Mistake

Aaron Collins

Aaron Collins is a former gang member serving a life-without-parole murder sentence at California State Prison in Sacramento. In the following viewpoint, Collins regrets his involvement with a Crips gang and his killing of a rival gang member. Collins maintains that after he acted on a fellow Crip's suggestion to kill the rival, that same gang member betrayed him by testifying against Collins at his murder trial.

As you read, consider the following questions:

1. How did Collins react upon being imprisoned?
2. What reason does the author give for feeling compelled to murder?
3. Whom does Collins blame for his fate?

Aaron Collins, "Gangbanger," *The Angolite*, September/October 1993. Reprinted with permission of Aaron Collins, #D-30738, PO Box 290066, Represa, CA 95671-0066.

How could I forget that rainy October afternoon when my freedom was savagely snatched by a courtroom of strangers? My body went limp when they found me guilty and sentenced me to spend the rest of my life behind concrete slabs and steel. On the way out, I stared into the audience and knew this would be the last time I'd be as close as this to my freedom. Two Hispanics shook their heads when they heard my sentence. They knew they were next because of similar crimes.

My attitude began to change. I began to feel that everybody was a snitch, and I wouldn't speak to anyone. My appetite declined, except for the sour taste of my dirty fingernails. I actually started to believe that God didn't exist, that He was a buster, punk, and straight-up joke. If He was real, He wouldn't have allowed those strangers to rape me of my freedom.

Behind Bars

The first time they closed the steel cage door on me, it was a "We got your ass forever" sound. It echoed as if mocking me for being so damn stupid. I tried to stay strong. I felt ridiculed, cut off from family, friends, and the whole damn world when my freedom was transferred to another man's hands. I gripped those steel bars as tight as I could. A single tear fell and descended slowly to the cold cell's floor. I couldn't hold on to my bravery and hardcore role any longer. A caravan of tears fell, each containing a different pain.

I cried myself into a short nap, no, more like a daze. I was young again, innocent and full of positive energy. And then I grew up fast, taking on the form and image of a ruthless gangbanger. My pants, any pants I wore, rested below the hump of my ass. I wore shirts two sizes larger than I needed, and my pockets were filled with money, drugs, and bullets. Inside my waistband was a friend I could always count on. His name was KILLER, better known as the Life-Taker.

Now that my eyes are open, I can't believe I was willing to die for a [gang] color, a damn meaningless color. Loved by few, hated by many was my slogan. I cared about nothing but my 'hood. And if it wasn't blue, it wasn't true. That's all I knew and wanted to know.

Sometimes me and the light would play games. I'd flick the light switch on and off, on and off, until I got tired or it wouldn't shine anymore.

And when I try to have peaceful dreams, I'm reminded of my crime. Immediately, a nightmare interrupts my dream starting with the night I took a life and ending with that damn steel cage door closing on me.

I took a life, an innocent life when I come to really think about it. I had to do it or be kicked off the set [gang]. I had to prove that I was down. I had to show everybody that I was hardcore. I had to prove that I was serious about Cripping and was willing to die for it. I did, too.

He called me Blood, a name that I ain't supposed to like. He challenged my dedication to my 'hood and disrespected my dead homeboys.

"Kill that fool," one of my homeboys yelled. I pulled out my best friend, aimed it at his head, closed my eyes, and squeezed the trigger one time. I heard his body fall to the concrete with such immense force. I watched as blood hid his entire face.

I looked around at my homeboy to get his approval, but he was gone. Everybody was gone.

I had followed his suggestion without making any of my own. It was he who made the decision for me. It was he who encouraged me to take the life of another human being. And it was he who took an oath, sat on the witness stand, and explained to the whole courtroom how I took a life—step by step.

A Choice

When I think about it, I mean really think about it, I had the opportunity to make my own decision, be my own man, and choose my own fate.

But now I'm sitting in a cold concrete cell, thinking about what would I do if I could do it all over again.

Three years have passed, and not once have I received a letter from my so-called homeboys. I did hear that two were killed; one became a member of our enemy gang. And my homeboy who took the stand on me has two children from my so-called girlfriend.

I like it here. I like to be told what to do and when to do it. I honestly love prison, because if I didn't, I would have made my own decision, chosen my own fate, and kept my ass at home. I don't blame nobody but me. How can I, when it was all my fault?

"Being in a gang is truly a positive thing, if you look at the loyalty, love and discipline that we have toward each other."

The Gang Life Is Worthwhile

Albert McGee

Albert McGee is a member of the Vice Lords, a predominantly black Chicago gang that dates back to the 1950s. In the following viewpoint, McGee asserts that the criminal justice system and the media rush to judge gang members negatively, regardless of the good they have done. McGee describes his acts of gang violence and argues that they were necessary to "survive the war" on the streets. McGee is incarcerated at the Mississippi State Penitentiary in Parchman for homicide and drug possession.

As you read, consider the following questions:

1. How does McGee describe his conduct in prison?
2. What reason does McGee give for joining the Vice Lords gang?
3. What does the author say about his mental state?

Albert McGee, "Ridin' Under the Five-Pointed Star," *Prison Life*, March 1995. Reprinted with permission.

We get all the bullshit just because we're in a gang. It doesn't matter what you're in for or how you handle your time behind bars.

Just about everybody in the system knows that the only thing you have to do is tell the police that a gang member has threatened your life and they'll go for it—because of all the bad press gang members get. Here in the Mississippi Department of Corrections [DOC], they don't give gang members a chance. If your name is brought up, you're assumed guilty until found otherwise.

It doesn't matter how much good I do. The fact that I'm a known gang member is enough. Forget that I'm going to college here. Forget that I've not had a rules violation report since I came here in '90. They look for the wrong in me, just because I'm a known gang member.

The Media

The media doesn't help; every time you turn around, you see something on the set about gang-related this or that. The media plays a big part in what the public thinks about gang members without even giving a person a chance for being human. The media is ignorant and the system is afraid.

If the DOC would let us talk to and handle our own, it would be better in here for the average guy. See, a lot of problems with gang members in prison is that older guys don't get a chance to talk to the young guys comin' in who are causing the most trouble. But the staff is afraid because they know we just might be able to do what they can't do.

I'm 33 years old and I've been an Insane Vice Lord for about 18 years. Like so many, I joined a gang at an early age. Contrary to popular belief, I didn't join because I lacked a family. For me, it was simply a matter of my surroundings. Had I lived about four blocks over, I would've been a Black Gangster Disciple instead of an Insane Vice Lord—which I'm very proud of being. I shall die a Vice Lord, loyal and true.

I've done some rather wild things, some of which I was never arrested for so I won't get too deep there. But I will try to let you see inside my mind.

There are some things, though, that can't be explained, like why I would want to take another's life for something as simple as a color. [Many gang members are distinguished by the particular color they wear.] I remember the first time I killed a rival gang member. I was 15 or 16 at the time; it was more of an act to prove myself than anything he did to me or any of my brothers. I stole a car and told myself that the first person I saw who's convenient I was gonna kill. After driving around some, there was this guy I saw going to his car. I just pulled up beside him and asked the time.

Then I shot him in the face with a .357 five times—being a Vice Lord I ride under the five-pointed star. After I shot him, I got out of my car and kicked him to make sure he was dead, which he was. Then I started dancing around and laughing, having a good ol' time. That was my first time, but not my last.

A Killing

Had the guy been with his brothers, I would have killed more of them 'cause killing a rival gang member was on my mind. When I saw him walking with the "flag" [bandanna displaying gang color] sticking out of his back pocket, I figured he may as well be a Gangster Disciple 'cause I shot him down like he was one. After that, I felt as though I could take on all them suckers. I even made a pact to try and kill, or at least just shoot, a gangster every few months or sooner if one of them did something, or if we just caught one or two of them off by themselves.

I once shot a rival's mother in both knees just to see how loud she could scream, especially since she thought I was going to kill her for sure.

Guess what I've always wanted to be? A serial killer, so they can make a movie or something about me. I know you're thinking I have no regard for others or myself, that I'm sick, or that I need help. Yes, maybe I do, but sometimes I just want someone to talk to, and someone to listen. Outside, I'm normal; but inside, only a select few really know who I am. I'm sick if you judge me by society's standards, but on the streets I'm just another gangbanger trying to survive the war.

Being in a gang is truly a positive thing, if you look at the loyalty, love and discipline that we have toward each other. The respect I have for other gang members is also deep, but hopefully we can all get together and stop some of the killing.

"All the gangs are armed. . . . Some gangs have a lot of guns, some a little bit."

Gangs Are Violent

Earl Shorris

Earl Shorris is a novelist and contributing editor for *Harper's Magazine*. In the following viewpoint, excerpted from his book *Latinos: A Biography of the People*, Shorris presents firsthand accounts by the Clarence Street gang in East Los Angeles. These gang members describe gangs' access to guns and the widespread violence among rival gangs. Clarence Street members also detail the beatings administered within their own gang.

As you read, consider the following questions:

1. For what reasons is the Clarence Street gang doubtful of peace among gangs?
2. What is the Clarence Street policy on drug use?
3. How does the gang decide to kick out a member, according to the author?

Like all people at the edge of the established world, the gangsters of East Los Angeles and El Chuco [El Paso, Texas] live abruptly; they decide with a glance who is a friend and who intends to kill them; there is no time for contemplation. If they guess wrong, there will always be someone to avenge a betrayal; that is the code and the comfort of the gang. . . .

In East Los Angeles

The victims of a failed immigration spoke of life in East L.A. It was late afternoon. The undocumented men were coming in after their day of labor, showering, playing cards, waiting for their simple meal of tortillas, cheese, and beans. A man recently released from prison tried to stop the fluid from leaking out of the transmission of his car. The police came by to taunt the gangsters, threatening them with the beatings they would administer in the dark. A girl who had recently been "jumped into" a gang walked around the churchyard showing off the bruises of the initiation. Someone was drunk; someone was stoned on marijuana. Everyone was talking and talking, kicking, proud to be gangsters, expecting some flare of life, a starburst. This is what [the Clarence Street gang] said:

J: No *veteranos* [veteran gang members] in our 'hood. All dead or in prison.

K: I'm in charge of the guns, and I have it right here. When everybody leaves, we take those guns, we hide 'em somewhere, only we know where it's at. We don't tell everybody, because then word gets out and somebody else might just come and get it and it'll be gone.

All the gangs are armed. Maybe they won't have a lot of them, but at least they'll have one. Some gangs have a lot of guns, some a little bit.

Maybe they have more weapons, but we'll have more people shooting. See, like if we had ten guns and you have a war right here, everybody's gonna get a gun and shoot, but if we only have three or four, we'll just get them and shoot. Those guns, like the Uzis, those we have for fighting. We don't have 'em for like around here.

J: We get the money for the Uzis selling dope, selling drugs, thieving, people that work.

K: Like, whatever goods there is, it belongs to the neighborhood. Like, if I have a gun, I can't just use it and gang bang. You can't do that. The gun's for the neighborhood.

L: To tell you the truth, we don't know how to shoot. What we do is just point the gun and pull the trigger, that's it. We don't know how to shoot from far and aim at his head and hit him. We just point the gun and shoot. If we hit 'em, we hit 'em; if we don't, we don't. We don't practice.

K: I practiced with my cousin. We go way up there in the mountains. My cousin, he has rifles and pistols and everything. He has a 12 gauge, a 14, a 9 millimeter Uzi, AK47, three .22 rifles, and a 9 millimeter pistol. And if I really need a pistol, I could go to my cousin and he would lend me it, but I have to give it back. But if I lend it to [N] and he gets caught, when he gets caught, you know, it's the loss of a gun, and the gun's registered to my cousin, so only the stolen guns, he'll probably lend it to me, but not the ones that are registered.

L: I could use a gun that belongs to the neighborhood. Anybody could use it. We've been using their pistols, TMC [The Mob Crowd] and Clarence, because we're together. If I want to borrow his pistol, I say, "Hey man, lend me your pistol. Lend it to me, I'm gonna do my work, I'm under cover."

We know where to hide the guns; we know who to trust. We know who to talk to.

No Peace

J: We don't make peace because there's one gang that's always gonna say, "Well, like if there's gonna be one gang, it's gonna be our gang."

It's like us, see, us, TMC, and like other gangs. TMC say, "Let's make one gang, but let's call it TMC." I ain't gonna want to do that because I'm from one gang, and I'm gonna say, "Why don't we make the whole gang and put it under my name." And you're gonna say, "No," and then we'll just start arguing and start a war right there.

M: When you grow up with a name, you stick with it. You know, I been in my neighborhood for like two, three years, and I ain't gonna say just like that, "All right, I'm gonna be a TMC now." I ain't gonna do that. They ain't gonna do that. Some people been in five, four, three years, whatever. They ain't gonna say, "Let's make it Clarence," because they have pride.

J: We had a shootout right here at the park where we had like seven guns. We had another shootout over here. The East L.A.s [Dukes], they tried to roll up on us. I mean, we can't let nobody else come in a car and come walking, you know, like give us their neighborhood. This our neighborhood, we got to back it up. We shot at them.

Nobody got killed. A couple people got hit. Somebody got hit in the leg. My homeboy Ozzie, you didn't see him sitting down like that. He got shot about two weeks ago. They shot him right here [abdomen right] and it ended right here [abdomen left]. They opened him up and took the bullet out. He's all stitched up.

K: West Side, it's not that they're afraid. It's just that . . . they do a lot of drugs and when they're on into drugs, say my homeboy here jump your car and they're onto drugs, they'll be all drugged out, and say, "We'll go tomorrow or later on." Then tomorrow comes and they say, "Well, we'll go some other day." You know, they'll never come back.

Like us, none of us do drugs, you know. We smoke weed, that ain't really nothin', but you know we smoke dope and we get our ass whipped by all the homeboys. All the homeboys get together. We call that court.

You go to court because you're fucked up.

Everybody is the judge, the whole gang. Like, if he was from my neighborhood and now, my neighborhood say they don't want him, we'll get him out. We'll beat him up, what everybody says. What everybody says, "We're gonna fuck him up. We're gonna fuck him up." You know, it's just what everybody says. What the majority says.

L: We make up meetings and we're all together and, you know, one of the main heads, any of them could say, "All right, the meeting is for this and that. You have to pitch in money to buy some pistols and this and that, and do you think we should kick him out of the neighborhood, yes or no? Should we jump him out? What do you guys think of that?" And they say, "Aw, he's a punk, he's a punk. Naw, kick him out." If everybody says that, we beat his ass and get on home.

"A real gangsta is out on the streets making millions, buying up businesses . . . to help uplift our [gang]."

Gangs
Seek Progress

Laron Douglas

Laron Douglas is a member of the Black Gangster Disciples, a prominent gang in Chicago and nearby cities. In the following viewpoint, Douglas argues that his fellow gang members are devoted to helping each other reach their fullest potential. Douglas renounces gang violence, but defends drug dealing by the Gangster Disciples as a source of income. Douglas contends that selling drugs is a prime means of escaping poverty in the ghetto, enabling his peers to make money, buy businesses, and become more productive. Douglas is incarcerated at Mansfield Correctional Institution in Mansfield, Ohio.

As you read, consider the following questions:

1. According to Douglas, how did fellow gang members treat him?
2. What reason does the author give for his imprisonment?
3. How did Douglas's opinion toward violence change?

Laron Douglas, "In the Mind of a True Disciple," *Prison Life*, March 1995. Reprinted with permission.

It's been four years since I was last on the streets in my everyday uniform: a black sweatshirt with a long blue T-shirt up under it, a black leather tweed belt turned to the right with my all-black, hard-leg Levis saggin' to perfection, a black Pro-Model cap, also turned deep to the right, a turkish gold rope and a beautiful six-pointed star on my right index finger. This is what it was to be a member of the glorious Gangster Disciple Nation on the streets.

Organizations in the streets are worse than in the joint. There is easy access to artillery and explosives, but being in a nation doesn't make one a criminal. It just shows one how to be more productive. If a brother is not willing to die for any particular cause, then that brother is lost.

Reaching Full Potential

I was brought up in this glorious nation to help all my brothers grow and reach their fullest potential. Kickin' it on one of our strips called the Graveyard, this trip is a multi-million dollar industry—nuthin' but drug sales, 24 hours a day. We make all the money we can to uplift our glorious nation, and a lot of members are meeting their quotas.

But don't get me wrong. There are many incidents in which the opposition tries to infiltrate our business. Even though we ain't practicing that gangbangin' trip no more, we haven't forgotten how to war.

Now we're teaching knowledge and money as the keys to success. I see brothaz all the time comin' to the joint with that 'bangin' mentality. I try to teach them to get wise. Money is what's going on. Being in the joint ain't cool for a real gangsta, a real gangsta is out on the streets making millions, buying up businesses in the community to help uplift our nation. I try to show these guys reality and make them more aware so that in the future, they won't make the same mistake.

We are also trying to help educate others on all the negativity against gangs—and I speak only about the Gangsta Disciples, 'cause that's what I am and will always be.

The Gangsta Disciple Nation is not a gang but an organization. I've been part of this glorious nation since '84. I'm from Cleveland, Ohio, but in Cleveland, Disciples are the majority. I've lost a lot of brothaz in this nation due to gangbanging. I don't associate with nobody outside of my nation.

Plenty of Good

Being in this glorious organization has taught me a lot. I grew up without a father and I turned to my Disciple brothaz for love. They knew exactly how to treat a brotha and were always there for me, through thick and thin.

I came to the joint for a gang-related murder I did not do. The police said I was shootin' at a rival gang member (Vice Lords), that I missed him and killed someone else. The police stuck that bullshit on me, but my Disciple brothaz have hired me a good lawyer and investigator. Things are looking good so hopefully I'll be up and out of prison before you know it.

When I was young, it was cool to 'bang. But it got our nation nowhere. Now I'm older and smarter and more aware. The dope game is a way to get quick money, and the brothaz see this, you know, living in the ghetto. They don't have too much, and selling dope gives them the chance to have the finer things in life. See, some brothaz only know how to hustle, which is good, but the brothaz with the great minds, we need them in school and college so we can own more businesses and become more productive in society. We do appreciate legit professions, but living in the ghetto is hard so we got to start somewhere and move up.

A Change Is Needed

I know that here the love is thick and strong, and all my brothaz is going to keep it real with me no matter what. I got a lot of animosity toward the opposition 'cause they took plenty of my brothaz away. I've took some, too, but the 'bangin' shit got old and I got tired of visiting my brothaz in coffins, throwing a six-point star over the dead body, sheddin' tears, then going back to the Graveyard (our strip) and getting drunk, reminiscing about the brotha. Then a cold rage would come over me, and I'd throw my body up for revenge. We'd all strap up and go into enemy territory and take care of some of them. But now I'm tired of that. Shit, that's why I feel that the preservation of my nation depends on true brothaz who want a change.

*"Ever since I got in that gang I feel like . . .
you even look at me wrong or say something
smart—fight!"*

Gangs Promote
Youth Violence

"Benz," interviewed by Larry A. Monroe and Michelle A. Felgar

Fourteen-year-old "Benz" was a gang member and a public
school student in Cleveland, Ohio, who had a history of unpre-
dictable assaultive behavior, according to interviewers Larry A.
Monroe and Michelle A. Felgar. "Benz" was unable to be maintained in the city school district's own special programs and was
enrolled in a private program for his behavioral problems. He
was subsequently sent to a juvenile detention facility for one
year, then returned to the public school system. In the following
viewpoint, the youth explains why he joined a gang, his violent
behavior, and his relationship with his parents. Monroe, now a
teacher in East Cleveland, and Felgar are former staff members
of the Positive Education Program, the private rehabilitation
program in Cleveland at which "Benz" was enrolled.

As you read, consider the following questions:

1. What reason does "Benz" give for believing his gang would
   not let him quit?
2. According to the youth, why was he scheduled to appear in
   court?
3. How did "Benz" respond to punishment from his parents?

"Benz," interviewed by Larry A. Monroe and Michelle A. Felgar, *Journal of Emotional &
Behavioral Problems*, vol. 1, no. 1, Spring 1992 (currently titled *Reclaiming Children and
Youth: The Journal of Emotional & Behavioral Problems*; published quarterly by the National
Educational Service, 1610 W. Third St., Bloomington, IN 47402. For order information: 800-
733-6786. Reprinted with permission.

Monroe and Felgar: *How did you become a member of the gang?*

"Benz": At first they were spreading around that we were going to start one. Everybody just started calling meetings; when it's hot, everybody would be standing out on the corner talking and, you know, people were just calling meetings on certain days. So then they had a meeting at Patrick Henry [Middle School] at the track. So, we had a meeting up there and we started talking.

Was it simply a social group when it first started?

Not at first. It had a point, a purpose. We were getting together for a reason.

Crips and Bloods

What was the reason?

One reason was about slobs [derogatory name for members of the Bloods gang]. You know, Crips and Bloods and stuff. I guess the reason is to take out one another—Crips fighting Bloods, Bloods fighting Crips. Kill one of them, so they kill one. The goal is to eliminate Bloods. Another reason is I just be fighting all the time and I needed the backup. That's all I wanted to do at first. But then people started using knives and weapons and stuff, and I didn't want to get shot.

Did you have any bad feelings about fighting people you didn't know?

No, it just happened. I don't know how it happened. Let's say we're walking and somebody just looks at you, looking you up and down and I'd say, "What you looking at, bitch?" Most of the time it's the rags. The blue or red. Red stands for Bloods, blue stands for Crips, and black stands for Folks.

Who are the Folks?

That's like another set of the Crips, like the Shotgun Crips.

Do they fight each other?

No, they fight together mostly, but sometimes they have their differences. Like, I had a difference with one. That's when I was in the hospital and I had fought one then. I didn't know 'til after, you know, he had a gun, but it wasn't loaded. That's one thing that upset me. And another thing, I kept leaving, then coming back. I wasn't consistently a member, you know. It was one Crip set against another Crip set. They were talkin' mess, you know. "This our territory, you trying to take over our territory."

So, what good came out of it? What did you get out of it?

Friends and stuff, you know. And sometimes it was fun going out together to the mall and stuff. Then, you know, they started shooting, just driving by and shooting. They'd shoot an innocent person just because they had red on.

Does that happen a lot here?

It happens here. When they were talking about those shootings on the news, that's what it was. Like at Heights, that was between the Betas and Kappas against MOB [Men Over Boys]. I know the boy who did the shooting. The head of that gang used to be called S——.

Avoiding Gangs

If you had a younger brother. . . .
I do.
Okay, if he came to you and told you he was going to join a gang, what would you do?
I wouldn't let him. No matter what happened, I wouldn't let him. I couldn't say what I would do, but I would do everything in my power not to let him get into it.
What would you tell him would happen if he joined?
He'd end up dead somewhere. He'll get shot. I know, I got into it because all my friends were in it and, you know, they wouldn't let me out of it. Still, I'm not out, you know. I just don't go nowhere when they go. I associate with some of them, but don't be in none of the activities. Like, if you have on a red or blue searag, you get arrested. They'll take you in for questioning.
Your friends who are not in gangs, how do they manage to stay out?
They just get out of the way, you know, go somewhere else.
If you had this to do all over again, would you?
No. You know, there was a lot of stuff I was doing, I just didn't get caught.
Why would they not let you out of the gang?
I think it's because you were in the gang, you know where their meetings were, you know what's going on, you know how they do things. If you leave one gang and go in another one, they would try to kill you if they find you. Because you could tell other people how they do things.

Making Money

Can you make money being in a gang?
When selling drugs there's some places you can't go or you'll get jumped. But if you're in the gang, wouldn't nobody mess with you. Nobody would jump you because you go get your boys and you'll be back. That's why I got into it, you know, for backup. So if I get in a fight or something or get jumped, they there. Another reason is that everybody was just doing it.
Do you have to give any of the money you make to the gang?
Not really, you know, unless you're trying to buy something. Like, we were all putting money in for a van or pickup truck; that was going to be our drive-by van.
Where do you get the drugs to sell?
You get the drugs anywhere.

Does the gang supply you with the drugs to sell?

It depends, some do, some don't. It depends what they are into. Some gangs just do robberies, some just fight. Like, that's how it used to be, just fighting, going to parties, tripping out and stuff. But then they got all serious, got in big time, started messing with the wrong people.

What do you feel could be done to stop this from happening?

You might as well not even try. You can never stop gangs.

Perhaps, but what can be done to stop the killing?

You can't stop them, you know. 'Cause now there's second generations. You can't stop it. You just can't stay still. They just want to be with the crowd like everybody else. You know, they want to be somebody, be popular, give you an identity.

Do you think if your parents were able to buy you those things, do you think you would have joined the gang anyway?

Really, yes, for the friendship. I don't know really. You could have all the money in the world and you would still join the gang. I know people that are in the gang who don't sell drugs, you know, they just like regular people. All got jobs and kids and stuff. They have like two lives.

Pulling Guns

How old is the oldest person in the gang?

Twenty-something, I guess. You know when you're in the gang it'll never be boring. You're always doing something, you're active, you know. It's fun when you're with a lot of people, and people see it. It gives you a reputation. I know a lot of people that if you mess with them you'll get shot. A lot of people got guns and pull them on people. I've pulled a gun on a lot of people, not to kill them, you know, just to scare them.

Were you ever afraid that they were going to pull one on you?

No.

Why not?

If I pulled a gun out on you, you wouldn't be thinking about moving. 'Cause if I had a loaded gun and you move, I'd shoot you right there.

And if you shoot me and I fall and come back up with a gun of my own?

I'd be one scared n——. I'd run.

But you never thought of it going that far?

No, but I could just shoot you again. If you get shot, you not going to get back up.

Are any of your friends from the gang in jail?

A lot is in jail. This boy named T——, he in jail for a year. This boy named B—— is in for life about, not life, like two years or something like that 'cause he shot some dog in the face. Shooting at stop signs, shooting at trees, at cars, shot somebody in the

167

back.

Compare yourself before the gang and after. Before the gang you were . . . ?

Civilized. I wouldn't be in all this trouble if I wasn't in the gang. You know, ever since I got in that gang I feel like, you know, you even look at me wrong or say something smart— fight! I just want to hit someone!

Do you want to talk about court?

I'll talk about it. ["Benz" faced charges in court the following day.]

Is the gang activity the cause of this court hearing?

It was, you know, promoted by the gang. Like that incident at P.H. [Patrick Henry]. I was with some members of the gang when I hit that teacher.

If you had been there without your fellow gang members, would you have hit him?

I wouldn't have hit him. I wouldn't have even been in there. But I know they're going to bring up all this stuff in school and all those other charges since I've been with the gang.

How long have you been involved with the gang?

Since last summer, about a year.

Do you think that your behavior in school has gotten worse because of your affiliation with the gang?

Yes. I'm not trying to blame it on something, but yes. You used to doing what you want in the streets, so. . . .

So, if you were not in a gang, what would your purpose be?

My purpose would be to just chill out. I can't stand to be locked up, I like my freedom.

Relations with Parents

Do your parents understand you?

No. I don't relate to them. I can't talk to them. I don't know why. Sometimes I can talk to my mother. But, you know, I give her little hints and sometimes she'll catch on. But I just don't talk to them. I'd probably get in trouble for it.

Does she ever come to you and ask you if you need some help, need to talk?

Sometimes, but I just . . . she knows when I'm lying.

Why do you feel you have to lie?

I just don't talk to my parents like that. I'm just, you know, scared to.

Did you get punished a lot by your parents?

Yeah, I got a lot of lickings. I got used to them—I used to like them [lickings] and I told them [parents]. Then they got tired and stopped. At least they were smart; they were just wasting their time. It don't hurt no more. But, you know, they didn't do nothing wrong raising me.

Would some positive feedback have made you feel better?

Sometimes, but it felt good in a way. They don't even talk about me getting sent [to a correctional facility].

Do you think they're afraid to talk about it?

Probably. My father probably knows I'm in a gang, but I don't know.

Do you feel that they are afraid of you because you're in a gang?

No, my parents'll kick my butt. If I try to hit him [father], I'll get shot.

So, what are you going to do when all of this is over?

I ain't getting in no more trouble. I ain't fighting, period. I'm just going to walk away. Like, I tried walking away once and got my whole face bashed. I'll just, you know, mellow out, stay with the girls like I was. The only trouble you can get into with girls is kids and that ain't nothing.

Taking care of children is "nothing"?

No, it's easy. Just get a job. I would like to drive a truck. I wouldn't get on welfare; I hate that. I wouldn't want my kid growing up in need. I'd talk to him, I'd give him money so he wouldn't get involved. Like, most people that sell drugs . . . like, I started because I needed the money.

What did you need the money for?

Pocket money. Like, my boys were at the store buying stuff. I couldn't buy nothing. When I was selling drugs I was making more money than he was (pointing to Mr. Monroe). I was bringing [drugs] to school and then I decided to stop.

Do you feel it is absolutely necessary to fight growing up in the inner-city?

Yes, 'cause if you don't, then people just going to take advantage of you and run all over you.

"This being respected stuff is really what's fucking up this world. . . . It's not just me, it's not just this neighborhood, it's every neighborhood."

Gang Members Create Fear to Gain Respect

"Twace"

When interviewed, "Twace," a Puerto Rican male, was a twenty-one-year-old convicted felon and recovering heroin addict in Brooklyn, New York. In the following viewpoint, "Twace" links his involvement with gangs, violence, and drugs to a powerful desire for gaining respect from others around him. "Twace" contends that virtually nothing stood in his way to build respect and his reputation. But he asserts that what he considered respect toward him was actually fear. "Twace" concludes that either imprisonment, drug addiction, or death awaits others seeking respect through crime and violence.

As you read, consider the following questions:

1. What does "Twace" say he liked about his drug use?
2. What was the author's attitude toward playing children's games and sports?
3. According to "Twace," why did his elders avoid his degree of crime and violence?

I first started using drugs, joining gangs, and running with the crowd when I was about nine years old.

I was running with clubs and stuff like that 'cause that gives you some kind of respect. But it was really kind of hard. Respect is something that you could lose at any moment, you know, you could lose it to stupidity. Sometimes I'm scared of myself because I know a few motherfuckin' things, from a gun to a knife. So sometimes it scares me, but it's the only way I know how to be.

I was going to a school where all these kids are crazy, everybody's using drugs, and you want to fit in. So by the time I went to junior high school I was already thirteen years old and I was somebody. I eventually ended up stabbing somebody, ended up shooting somebody and using drugs. . . .

Carrying Weight

So I went to school and I was already a murderer and this carried a lot of weight. I was somebody, all the girls liked me, man. I was a little king to all those girls.

Then I started getting into heavier stuff. And this is all because of the reputation. This is all 'cause you want to be somebody, because you gotta be down. Your name has gotta ring. And if your name don't ring, you ain't nobody. . . .

You know, everybody who had a reputation, somebody follows him so they can be somebody, so I carried a lot of people, man. I carry a lot of people to this day. I got hurt, I've been arrested, I've been in jail for protecting a lot of different people.

I started popping pills like crazy. I started doing a lot of 'ludes, a lot of quaaludes. I mean, I didn't even know what I was on, I was so wiped out of my head. I just did it because I liked the way I looked when I was high—I looked like I was a maniac, I looked like I was crazy. Nobody would dare fuck with me. I used to go to school, the teachers were scared of me, you know. I rang bells. I got through two junior high schools because of fear. The principals used to fear me, the police used to fear me. It was all because I had to prove something and I was willing to prove it even if I got killed.

Even to this day, sometimes I be scared of myself, because I could be killed at any time or moment just because I don't give a flying fuck because I can't be disrespected. I can't be disrespected and that's the way I live.

Then I switched schools and one day I see these guys walking past and they dared my cousin and I said, Yo, man, you dare me to be down with them people? I'll give you five minutes. And he was like, Yeah, I dare you. So I went over and I joined them. I had to whack the shit out of some guy with a chain. I mean I almost killed the guy.

I almost killed the poor guy, but then after that it was all right,

I was down with the posse. Mutual respect again like I needed it, you know what I mean? I joined the club because I needed the respect. Wherever I went I didn't want nobody to bother me, and the only club in this school that had everybody in control was these people. So I run down with them.

Fear, Not Respect

This is when I started doing the heaviest drugs there is. It's heroin and I'm only fifteen years old. I usually say it was the love of my life. But, you know, you think 'cause you look down, and you think 'cause you look crazy, people will respect you, but they just scared of you, it's not respect. It's just being scared. Plain bloody scared.

When you're on these missions, people are just scared of you, but it's not because they look at that dude and say, Oh, man, I respect this guy. This guy did this. This guy helped this person. This guy helped build this. You know. Nah, if anything, I might help somebody tear something down and do something to somebody. To hurt them. It's all fear. It's all fear. I mean at times it feels good, sometimes, but sometimes it doesn't. . . .

One time, I was seventeen and I was coming from work. I'm not lazy, I do like to work. I work when I have to. This time I had a car, so I had to work. I had to afford the gas and all that stuff. And I had this girl, it's when I first had my kid. So I'm driving and I see this dude from a club that I didn't like. This was something that went back to when I was thirteen years old. I see this guy with his arm wrapped around my little sister, and I drive up. I'm carrying a bag. You carry a bag in case you have a problem with somebody.

I pick up the bag, he gives me a smile, like what am I going to do. What am I going to do? I'm a guy who's being raced up, being respected. Nobody will look at my face, nobody will smile at my face unless I am smiling. Nobody would even talk to me unless I talked to them. Now this guy goes smiling in my face. First thing I react to was to kill him, you know what I mean? You gonna laugh at me, I'm gonna kill you. And that's basically what I almost did. . . .

The Need for Respect Is Everywhere

I was just raised like this, you know. This being respected stuff is really what's fucking up this world. The youth of the world. 'Cause it's everywhere, this is not just me, you know. This is a problem with everybody. It's not just me, it's not just this neighborhood, it's every neighborhood, from blacks to Puerto Ricans to white boys to Chinks to everything. There's always got to be a leader.

Always got to be a leader and I was willing to be the leader.

Sometimes my brothers, my homeboys, my friends, they would say, Twace, you gotta chill out, 'cause one day you're gonna get killed. There's going to be a guy who maybe is crazier than you who's going to take you out.

I didn't care. I didn't give a flying fuck, you know. To this day I'd be scared of myself because I know how I am. The problem is having this respect, this thing we're supposed to have. When I look at my father or my uncles and stuff, they don't act the way I act. They never been down with that. I didn't play tag and all that shit. I thought that was for punks. What I was doing was crazy, way crazier. The people I ran with wasn't doing stupidities like that. I figured it was stupid—hide-and-go-seek, playing tag, man hunting, and all this kiddie shit. I mean I don't even know how to play that stuff. I don't know nothing about playing football or basketball or baseball 'cause I never spend no time with it. I spend time with my self-rep, you know, building up my reputation. . . .

Respect in Jail

In jail, Puerto Rican is German. German mean Nazi, like outlaw, crazy motherfucker, willing to cut anybody up, willing to just kill somebody. And the people I was with, they were punks, Puerto Rican guys I was with were punks. So I was on my own basically, sixty-some guys to a dorm. I had to rip a couple of people up, you know. And after that people were doing me stuff, people begging me so they can clean my clothes for a cigarette.

When you're in there, you got to have the respect you had in the street. Because you could be—I mean, the guys that were in prison were nothing but a bunch of suckers. And out here they thought they were hot shit. To this day they see me and they don't even look at me because they're degraded, you know. . . .

A Heroin Habit

Time went by and I ended up [out of jail] using drugs all over again. I was lifting weights. Started using drugs and building myself up. *Boom.* Became a junkie. This time it was no more about being respected. I mean I was a junkie and I was respected 'cause people would think back, Man, if he was this crazy way back, he's crazy now, you know what I mean, 'cause you can't be a punk once and be a bad motherfucker again. I mean you a bad motherfucker, or you just ain't. I was the meanest junkie that was around here. I would have robbed anybody, stabbed anybody, shot anybody, in a matter of a heartbeat. Heroin is something very big. It's not a dictator of your mind, it's a dictator of your body. . . .

This is something that my respect brought me to, you know.

To becoming a heroin addict. I'm not proud of it, but I'm also not ashamed of it. I figure it was something that I had to go through to learn what life was really about, you know. . . .

Nothing but a Dead End

To this day I wish that something I say will scare somebody away from doing what I did, man, 'cause what I did wasn't worth it. I spent my whole childhood, my whole childhood in and out of prison. I was high out of my head. I had a lot of friends I grew up with, but the only one who ever gave me drugs was me. And this was because I had to be somebody, somebody that people respected, man.

That's the bottom line, *boom*, for every whopper [important person] out there there's a tomb, for every whopper there's a cell, for every whopper out there there's a drug's box [coffin]. 'Cause there's only three ways you going, man: You going to jail, you going to be killed, or you're going to be a dope fiend, crackhead, whatever it is, because it's all in the game. It's all in the game of this respect bullshit. I look at my elders, man, they never went through stuff like this, 'cause they didn't have to prove nothing to nobody. In those days it was, I don't know, I really can't say what it was like in those days, but it sure in hell was better than it is now, man.

Periodical Bibliography

The following articles have been selected to supplement the diverse views presented in this chapter.

Barbara Cottman Becnel — "Stanley (Tookie) Williams: The Crips Co-founder Now Realizes Violence Does Not Solve Anything," *Los Angeles Times*, August 22, 1993. Available from Times Mirror Square, Los Angeles, CA 90012-3816.

Lewis Cole — "Hyper Violence," *Rolling Stone*, December 1, 1994.

Richard Lee Colvin — "Youngest Homeboy Wants Out," *Los Angeles Times*, July 24, 1993.

Sharin Elkholy and Ahmed Nassef — "Crips and Bloods Speak for Themselves: Voices from South Central," *Against the Current*, July/August 1992.

Jon D. Hull — "No Way Out," *Time*, August 17, 1992.

Stuart H. Isett — "From Killing Fields to Mean Streets," *World Press Review*, December 1994.

Jet — "Black Youths Tell How Gangs and Guns Have Them Planning Their Own Funerals," January 31, 1994.

Tina Luongo — "I Was a Gang Girl," *Mademoiselle*, July 1994.

Seth Mydans — "'Retired' and Regretting the Gang Life," *The New York Times*, June 14, 1994.

Richard Rodriguez — "Gangstas: Hard Truths from the Streets of East L.A.," *Mother Jones*, January/February 1994.

Sanyika Shakur — "Can't Stop, Won't Stop: The Education of a Crip Warlord," *Esquire*, April 1993.

Los Solidos Nation — "Family Values: The Gangster Version," *Harper's Magazine*, April 1995.

Don Terry — "Chicago's Gangs: Machiavelli's Descendants," *The New York Times*, September 18, 1994.

John Tierney — "Fernando, 16, Finds a Sanctuary in Crime," *The New York Times*, April 13, 1993.

Muriel L. Whitstone — "From the Jailhouse to the Statehouse," *Ebony*, January 1994.

For Further Discussion

Chapter 1

1. In her viewpoint, C. DeLores Tucker argues that gangsta rap music gives youths "false and hateful concepts about women" and that its sale to children should be banned. Do you agree with either or both of these statements? Why or why not? Do you believe that Tucker's position conflicts with the First Amendment's protection of free speech? Explain.

2. According to James M. O'Kane, ethnic minority criminals are eager to "make it big" in America and fulfill the American Dream, primarily through drug-dealing. Compare the backgrounds of immigrant criminals and U.S.-born citizens. Can you identify any economic or cultural forces influencing immigrants to seek wealth through crime? If so, explain these forces.

Chapter 2

1. D. Saccente and Jeffrey J. Mayer disagree that gangs are dangerous criminal enterprises. Does one or the other author make a stronger argument about the organizational structure of gangs? If so, why is it stronger? Evaluate the authors' sources of information. Which is more convincing? Why?

2. Joseph L. Albini argues that many Italians have been harmed by stereotypes of Mafia members. Do you believe similar stereotypes exist of inner-city minority gang members? If so, describe the stereotypes. Are these minority groups stigmatized, in your opinion?

Chapter 3

1. Ben Garza's teenage son was a gang member who was seriously injured in a drive-by shooting. Does this fact make you more likely to side with Garza against gangs? Why? The author stresses the need to increase opportunities for youths as alternatives to gang involvement. Make a list of Garza's suggestions as well as of your own, then rank them according to importance.

2. According to Greg Boyle, the availability of jobs, even those paying minimum wage, is a key to keeping youths away from gangs. Do you agree with Boyle that youths would prefer low-paying jobs to dealing drugs? Why or why not?

3. Luis J. Rodriguez argues that gang youths should not be incarcerated because it does nothing to solve the gang problem. What other punitive measures do you believe would help reform gang members? How effective would Rodriguez consider these measures to be? Explain.

4. Michael Genelin is a prosecutor in an antigang division of the Los Angeles district attorney's office. How is his affiliation reflected in his argument? Genelin supports an ordinance prohibiting gang members from entering a community park. Compare this ordinance with similar ones described by Terence R. Boga in his viewpoint. How reasonable do you consider the park ordinance to be? Why?

5. In his viewpoint, Terence R. Boga contends that gang members should be allowed to assemble peacefully in public places. Do you believe that such assembly constitutes a public threat? Why or why not? In your own neighborhood, would you support or oppose the rights of known gang members to assemble in public? Explain your reasoning.

Chapter 4

1. Albert McGee writes frankly about the enjoyment he took in drive-by shootings. Aaron Collins regrets shooting a rival gang member. Do you believe that a gang member's remorse, or lack thereof, should be considered by the justice system in meting out punishment? Explain your answer.

2. In his viewpoint, "Twace" describes his out-of-control desire for respect that resulted in violence, jail time, and a drug habit. Do you think there is any correlation between the environment of his inner-city neighborhood and his demand for respect? Explain. In what other ways could the author have sought respect?

Organizations to Contact

The editors have compiled the following list of organizations concerned with the issues debated in this book. The descriptions are derived from materials provided by the organizations. All have publications or information available for interested readers. The list was compiled on the date of publication of the present volume; names, addresses, and phone numbers may change. Be aware that many organizations take several weeks or longer to respond to inquiries, so allow as much time as possible.

American Civil Liberties Union (ACLU)
132 W. 43rd St.
New York, NY 10036
(212) 944-9800

The ACLU is a national organization that works to defend Americans' civil rights as guaranteed by the U.S. Constitution. It opposes curfew laws for juveniles and others and seeks to protect the public-assembly rights of gang members or people associated with gangs. The ACLU publishes the biannual newsletter *Civil Liberties*.

Boston Violence Prevention Program (BVPP)
1010 Massachusetts Ave., 2nd Fl.
Boston, MA 02118
(617) 534-5196

This program teaches counselors and trainers violence prevention strategies, which are then taught to the public in schools and community centers. Its projects include gang and drug prevention programs. BVPP publishes the bimonthly newsletter *Against the Tide*.

California Youth Authority Gang Violence Reduction Project (CYA-GVRP)
2445 N. Mariondale Ave., Suite 202
Los Angeles, CA 90032
(213) 227-4114
fax: (213) 227-5169

Operated by state parole agents, the project's goal is to mediate feuds among gangs in East Los Angeles. Its activities include developing job opportunities for former gang members, removing graffiti, and establishing parents groups. Staff members speak to organizations about prevention and other topics related to youth gangs. The project publishes pamphlets and a directory of organizations concerned with gangs.

Center for Democratic Renewal (CDR)
PO Box 50469
Atlanta, GA 30302-0469
(404) 221-0025

CDR is a national clearinghouse for information about the white supremacist movement in general and the Ku Klux Klan in particular. It works to end hate violence and bigotry and has participated in many First Amendment debates about the rights of hate groups versus the rights of groups targeted by them. It offers programs of education, research, victim assistance, community organizing, leadership training, and public policy advocacy. CDR publishes the bimonthly newsletter the *Monitor*, the manual *When Hate Groups Come to Town: A Handbook of Community Responses*, and an information packet on skinheads and neo-Nazis.

Center for the Study of Youth Policy
University of Pennsylvania School of Social Work
4200 Pine St., 2nd Fl.
Philadelphia, PA 19104-4090
(215) 898-2229
fax: (215) 573-2791

The center studies issues concerning juvenile justice and youth corrections. Although it does not take positions itself regarding these issues, it publishes individuals' opinions in booklets, including *Programs for Serious and Violent Juvenile Offenders* and *Violent Juvenile Crime: What Do We Know About It and What Can We Do About It?* The center also publishes the monograph *A Blueprint for Youth Corrections*.

Children of War
28 Windsor St.
Arlington, MA 02174
(617) 646-1276

Children of War is a youth leadership training program that encourages youths to play active roles in reversing violence. Children in the organization, which seeks to create local groups, are victims of war and gang violence who serve as peer role models, inspiring a sense of purpose and vision in young people. Children of War expects to have future publications available.

Gang and Youth Crime Prevention Program (GYCPP)
Ministry of Attorney General, Community Justice Branch
207-815 Hornby St.
Vancouver, BC, Canada V6Z 2E6
(604) 660-2605
hotline: (800) 680-4264 (British Columbia only)
fax: (604) 775-2674

This program works with government ministries, police, public agencies, community-based organizations, and youth in order to raise awareness, and reduce the incidence, of gang- and youth-related crime and violence. GYCPP maintains a youth violence directory, conducts community forums and school workshops, creates videos, and publishes a set of booklets on Canada's criminal justice system.

Gang Violence Bridging Project
Edmund G. "Pat" Brown Institute of Public Affairs
California State University, Los Angeles
5151 State University Dr.
Los Angeles, CA 90032-8261
(213) 343-3770
fax: (213) 343-3774

The project seeks to create bridges of communication among communities in the Los Angeles area. It advocates development of services and policies designed to prevent gang activity and provide alternatives to gang membership, as opposed to traditional suppressive measures such as incarceration. The project believes that the problem of gang violence must be addressed in the context of poverty, unemployment, and deteriorating schools and youth services. It publishes fact sheets on gang violence and related topics, a resource book on education spending and incarceration, and a periodic newsletter.

International Association of Chiefs of Police (IACP)
515 N. Washington St.
Alexandria, VA 22314
(703) 836-6767

The association consists of police executives who provide consultation and research services to, and support educational programs for, police departments nationwide. It publishes *Police Chief* magazine monthly, which covers all aspects of law enforcement duty, including gang prevention.

Milton S. Eisenhower Foundation
1660 L St. NW, Suite 200
Washington, DC 20036
(202) 429-0440

The foundation consists of individuals dedicated to reducing crime in inner-city neighborhoods through community programs. It believes that more federally funded programs such as Head Start and Job Corps would improve education and job opportunities for youths, thus reducing juvenile crime and violence. The foundation's publications include the report *Youth Investment and Community Reconstruction* and the monthly newsletter *Challenges from Within*.

National Council for Urban Economic Development (NCUED)
1730 K St. NW, Suite 915
Washington, DC 20006
(202) 223-4735

The council consists of business and economic development professionals and corporations interested in city development. It advocates federal aid to cities and supports enterprise zones as a means to stimulate inner-city economies. It publishes the quarterly magazine *Commentary* and the semimonthly newsletter *Economic Developments*.

National Council on Crime and Delinquency (NCCD)
685 Market St., Suite 620
San Francisco, CA 94105
(415) 896-6223
fax: (415) 896-5109

NCCD supports crime prevention programs aimed at strengthening families, reducing school dropout rates, and increasing employment opportunities for low-income youth. It opposes placing minors in adult jails and executing those who have committed capital offenses before the age of eighteen. It publishes the quarterly journal *Crime and Delinquency*, the quarterly *FOCUS Research Briefs*, and policy papers, including *Reducing Crime in America: A Pragmatic Approach*.

National Crime Prevention Council (NCPC)
1700 K St. NW, 2nd Fl.
Washington, DC 20006-3817
(202) 466-6272
fax: (202) 296-1356

NCPC provides training and technical assistance to groups and individuals interested in crime prevention. It advocates job training and recreation programs as means to reduce youth crime and violence. The council, which sponsors the Take a Bite Out of Crime campaign, publishes the book *Preventing Violence: Program Ideas and Examples*, the booklet *Violence, Youth, and a Way Out*, and the newsletter *Catalyst*, which is published ten times a year.

National Institute Against Prejudice and Violence (NIAPV)
712 W. Lombard St.
Baltimore, MD 21201
(410) 706-5170

The institute studies the problem of violence and intimidation motivated by racial, religious, ethnic, or sexual prejudice. It believes that youth crimes are a serious problem and that parents, clergy, and youth counselors can reduce this problem by helping to dispel harmful stereotypes of ethnic, religious, and minority groups and by teaching young people how to resolve conflict peacefully. NIAPV publishes the quarterly newsletter *Forum*.

National Institute of Justice (NIJ)
PO Box 6000
Rockville, MD 20849-6000
(800) 851-3420

NIJ is the primary federal sponsor of research on crime and its control. It sponsors research efforts through grants and contracts that are carried out by universities, private institutions, and state and local agencies. Its publications include the research briefs *Gang Crime and Law Enforcement Recordkeeping* and *Street Gang Crime in Chicago*.

National School Safety Center (NSSC)
4165 Thousand Oaks Blvd., Suite 290
Westlake Village, CA 91362
(805) 373-9977

Part of Pepperdine University, the center is a research organization that studies school crime and violence, including gang and hate crimes, and that provides technical assistance to local school systems. NSSC believes that teacher training is an effective way of reducing juvenile crime. It publishes the booklet *Gangs in Schools: Breaking Up Is Hard to Do* and the *School Safety Update* newsletter, published nine times a year.

Office of Juvenile Justice and Delinquency Prevention (OJJDP)
PO Box 6000
Rockville, MD 20849-6000
(800) 638-8736

As the primary federal agency charged with monitoring and improving the juvenile justice system, OJJDP develops and funds programs on juvenile justice. Among its goals are the prevention and control of illegal drug use and serious juvenile crime. Through its Juvenile Justice Clearinghouse, OJJDP distributes fact sheets and reports such as *Gang Suppression and Intervention* and *Juvenile Intensive Supervision*. It publishes the *OJJDP Juvenile Justice Bulletin* periodically.

Youth Crime Watch of America (YCWA)
9300 S. Dadeland Blvd., Suite 100
Miami, FL 33156
(305) 670-2409
fax: (305) 670-3805

YCWA is a nonprofit, student-led organization that promotes crime and drug prevention programs in communities and schools throughout the United States. Member-students at the elementary and secondary level help raise others' awareness concerning alcohol and drug abuse, crime, gangs, guns, and the importance of staying in school. Strategies include organizing student assemblies and patrols, conducting workshops, and challenging students to become personally involved in preventing crime and violence. YCWA publishes the quarterly newsletter *National Newswatch*.

Bibliography of Books

Felix Aguirre — *A Parent's Guide to Street Gangs.* San Diego: Marin, 1993.

Joseph L. Albini — *The American Mafia: Genesis of a Legend.* New York: Irvington, 1971.

Richard Arthur with Edsel Erickson — *Gangs and Schools.* Holmes Beach, FL: Learning Publications, 1992.

Léon Bing — *Do or Die.* New York: HarperCollins, 1991.

Anne Campbell — *The Girls in the Gang.* 2nd ed. Cambridge, MA: Blackwell, 1991.

Richard C. Cervantes, ed. — *Substance Abuse and Gang Violence.* Newbury Park, CA: Sage, 1992.

Loren Christensen — *Skinhead Street Gangs.* Boulder, CO: Paladin, 1994.

Herbert C. Covey, Scott Menard, and Robert Franzese — *Juvenile Gangs.* Springfield, IL: Charles C. Thomas, 1992.

Scott Cummings and Daniel J. Monti, eds. — *Gangs: The Origins and Impact of Contemporary Youth Gangs in the United States.* Albany: State University of New York Press, 1993.

David Dawley — *A Nation of Lords: The Autobiography of the Vice Lords.* 2nd ed. Prospect Heights, IL: Waveland, 1992.

Shirley Dicks, ed. — *Young Blood: Juvenile Justice and the Death Penalty.* Buffalo: Prometheus, 1995.

Rose M. Duhon-Sells, ed. — *Dealing with Youth Violence: What Schools and Communities Need to Know.* Bloomington, IN: National Education Service, 1995.

Miguel Duran — *Don't Spit on My Corner.* Houston: Arte Publico Press, 1992.

T.J. English — *Born to Kill: The True Story of America's Most Notorious Vietnamese Gang.* New York: William Morrow, 1995.

Diego Gambetta — *The Sicilian Mafia: The Business of Private Protection.* Cambridge: Harvard University Press, 1993.

Arnold P. Goldstein and C. Ronald Huff, eds. — *The Gang Intervention Handbook.* Champaign, IL: Research Press, 1993.

Arnold P. Goldstein and Barry Glick, with Wilma Carthan and Douglas A. Blancero
The Prosocial Gang: Implementing Aggression Replacement Therapy. Newbury Park, CA: Sage, 1994.

John M. Hagedorn
People and Folks: Gangs, Crime, and the Underclass in a Rustbelt City. Chicago: Lake View Press, 1988.

Gregory M. Herek and Kevin T. Berrill
Hate Crimes: Confronting Violence Against Lesbians and Gay Men. Newbury Park, CA: Sage, 1992.

Maria Hinojosa
Crews: Gang Members Talk to Maria Hinojosa. San Diego: Harcourt Brace, 1995.

C. Ronald Huff, ed.
Gangs in America. Newbury Park, CA: Sage, 1990.

Martin Sanchez Jankowski
Islands in the Street: Gangs and Urban American Society. Berkeley and Los Angeles: University of California Press, 1991.

Darryl Johnson
This Thing Called Gangs: A Guide to Recognizing the Danger Signs. Topeka, KS: Lone Tree, 1992.

George W. Knox
An Introduction to Gangs. Rev. ed. Bristol, IN: Wyndham Hall, 1994.

Joan W. Moore
Going Down to the Barrio: Homeboys and Homegirls in Change. Philadelphia: Temple University Press, 1991.

James M. O'Kane
The Crooked Ladder: Gangsters, Ethnicity, and the American Dream. New Brunswick, NJ: Transaction, 1992.

Felix M. Padilla
The Gang as an American Enterprise. New Brunswick, NJ: Rutgers University Press, 1992.

Deborah Prothrow-Stith
Deadly Consequences: How Violence Is Destroying Our Teenage Population. New York: HarperCollins, 1991.

Peter Reuter, Robert MacCoun, and Patrick Murphy
Money from Crime: A Study of the Economics of Drug Dealing in Washington, D.C. Santa Monica, CA: RAND Corp., 1990.

Luis J. Rodriguez
Always Running: La Vida Loca: Gang Days in L.A. Willimantic, CT: Curbstone, 1993.

Sandy Sadowsky with H.B. Gilmour
Wedded to Crime: My Life in the Jewish Mafia. New York: Putnam, 1992.

William B. Sanders
Gangbangs and Drive-bys: Grounded Culture and Juvenile Gang Violence. New York: Aldine de Gruyter, 1994.

Sanyika Shakur   *Monster: The Autobiography of an L.A. Gang Member.* New York: Penguin, 1994.

Earl Shorris   *Latinos: A Biography of the People.* New York: Norton, 1992.

Bob Sipchen   *Baby Insane and the Buddha: How a Crip and a Cop Joined Forces to Shut Down a Street Gang.* New York: Doubleday, 1993.

Claire Sterling   *Thieves' World: The Threat of the New Global Network of Organized Crime.* New York: Simon & Schuster, 1994.

Mercer L. Sullivan   *"Getting Paid": Youth Crime and Work in the Inner City.* Ithaca, NY: Cornell University Press, 1989.

Carl S. Taylor   *Dangerous Society.* East Lansing: Michigan State University Press, 1989.

Carl S. Taylor   *Girls, Gangs, Women, and Drugs.* East Lansing: Michigan State University Press, 1993.

Frederick L. Thrasher *The Gang: A Study of 1,313 Gangs in Chicago.* Chicago: University of Chicago Press, 1927.

U.S. House of Repre-   *Threat of International Organized Crime.* Wash-
sentatives Committee   ington: Government Printing Office, 1994.
on Foreign Affairs

U.S. Senate   *Recent Developments in Transnational Crime
Committee on   Affecting U.S. Law Enforcement and Foreign Pol-
Foreign Relations   icy.* Washington: Government Printing Office, 1994.

U.S. Sentencing   *Violent Crimes/Firearms/Gangs Working Group
Commission   Report.* Washington: U.S. Sentencing Commission, 1992.

James Diego Vigil   *Barrio Gangs: Street Life and Identity in Southern California.* Austin: University of Texas Press, 1988.

Margot Webb   *Coping with Street Gangs.* Rev. ed. New York: Rosen, 1992.

William F. Whyte   *Street Corner Society: The Social Structure of an Italian Slum.* 4th ed. Chicago: University of Chicago Press, 1993.

Terry Williams   *The Cocaine Kids: The Inside Story of a Teenage Drug Ring.* Reading, MA: Addison-Wesley, 1989.

Index